THE MUTUAL FUNDS BOOK:

How to Invest in Mutual Funds & Earn High Rates of Returns Safely

By Alan Northcott

THE MUTUAL FUNDS BOOK: HOW TO INVEST IN MUTUAL FUNDS & EARN HIGH RATES OF RETURNS SAFELY

Copyright © 2009 Atlantic Publishing Group, Inc.
1405 SW 6th Avenue • Ocala, Florida 34471 • Phone 800-814-1132 • Fax 352-622-1875
Web site: www.atlantic-pub.com • E-mail: sales@atlantic-pub.com
SAN Number: 268-1250

Northcott, Alan, 1951-
  The mutual funds book : how to invest in mutual funds & earn high rates of returns / by Alan Northcott.
    p. cm.
Includes bibliographical references and index.
ISBN-13: 978-1-60138-001-2 (alk. paper)
ISBN-10: 1-60138-001-1 (alk. paper)
1. Mutual funds. 2. Portfolio management. 3. Investments. I. Title.
HG4530.N665 2009
332.63'27--dc22

                              2009027205

Printed in the United States

PROJECT MANAGER: Melissa Peterson • mpeterson@atlantic-pub.com
COVER & JACKET DESIGN: Holly Marie Gibbs • hgibbs@atlantic-pub.com
INTERIOR DESIGN: Samantha Martin • smartin@atlantic-pub.com
ASSISTANT EDITOR: Angela Pham • apham@atlantic-pub.com

Printed on Recycled Paper

We recently lost our beloved pet "Bear," who was not only our best and dearest friend but also the "Vice President of Sunshine" here at Atlantic Publishing. He did not receive a salary but worked tirelessly 24 hours a day to please his parents. Bear was a rescue dog that turned around and showered myself, my wife, Sherri, his grandparents Jean, Bob, and Nancy, and every person and animal he met (maybe not rabbits) with friendship and love. He made a lot of people smile every day.

We wanted you to know that a portion of the profits of this book will be donated to The Humane Society of the United States.   *—Douglas & Sherri Brown*

The human-animal bond is as old as human history. We cherish our animal companions for their unconditional affection and acceptance. We feel a thrill when we glimpse wild creatures in their natural habitat or in our own backyard.

Unfortunately, the human-animal bond has at times been weakened. Humans have exploited some animal species to the point of extinction.

The Humane Society of the United States makes a difference in the lives of animals here at home and worldwide. The HSUS is dedicated to creating a world where our relationship with animals is guided by compassion. We seek a truly humane society in which animals are respected for their intrinsic value, and where the human-animal bond is strong.

Want to help animals? We have plenty of suggestions. Adopt a pet from a local shelter,

join The Humane Society and be a part of our work to help companion animals and wildlife. You will be funding our educational, legislative, investigative and outreach projects in the U.S. and across the globe.

Or perhaps you'd like to make a memorial donation in honor of a pet, friend or relative? You can through our Kindred Spirits program. And if you'd like to contribute in a more structured way, our Planned Giving Office has suggestions about estate planning, annuities, and even gifts of stock that avoid capital gains taxes.

Maybe you have land that you would like to preserve as a lasting habitat for wildlife. Our Wildlife Land Trust can help you. Perhaps the land you want to share is a backyard— that's enough. Our Urban Wildlife Sanctuary Program will show you how to create a habitat for your wild neighbors.

So you see, it's easy to help animals. And The HSUS is here to help.

2100 L Street NW • Washington, DC 20037 • 202-452-1100
www.hsus.org

DEDICATION

"Dedicated to my beautiful wife, Liz, my constant companion through life's adventures and my strength for more than 30 years."

TABLE OF CONTENTS

Chapter 3: What Other Fund Investments Are Available?   55

Chapter 4: Underlying Investments in a Fund   61

Chapter 5: Checking Up on Fund Performance   83

Chapter 10: How Can I Choose From So Many? 165

Chapter 11: Assembling a Portfolio 181

Chapter 12: Sample Portfolio Selection 199

Chapter 13: Advanced Techniques to Increase Yield 223

CHAPTER 1

Introduction to Mutual Funds

If you are like many people, you might believe you already know what mutual funds are, and you are reading this book to help you decide which to invest in. But if you have not researched mutual funds before, you may be surprised by the range and number available, and it will be worth your while to discover the variety you can invest your money in.

Simply put, mutual funds are a means to invest in something along with other people. The advantage this offers over investing your money individually is having a professional fund manager whose job is to look after the invested funds and make any necessary adjustments according to his or her knowledge and experience. The mutual fund, as a whole, amounts to more money than you could invest alone, which may open up possibilities for investment by a manager who can produce greater returns. The large size of the portfolio means that the manager can diversify the holdings more than you could on your own, which spreads the risk.

There are a wide range of potential purchases for the manager. It is not as simple as just buying some stocks or bonds; there are many variations available for the mutual fund manager to choose from, and you will select the fund and management according to both the level of risk you find acceptable and your ideal return. You can invest in money market funds, income funds, growth funds, value funds, index funds, sector funds, international funds, and other permutations. Successful investing takes time, and you will find that, overall, the price you pay for professional management is relatively cheap compared with the value that you will receive.

The History of Mutual Funds

For as long as people have had markets to invest in, groups of people have banded together to combine their money and expertise to make better returns. The mutual fund is a logical extension of this idea, in which the investors pay someone to manage their money and commit the time to research investments, resulting in more informed investing.

In the 19th century in the United Kingdom, organizations called investment trusts sold shares to investors. This was the likely origin of a company looking after investors' money, and the idea was adopted in the United States in 1924. Many of the first funds were closed-end funds, meaning there were a certain number of shares for sale that were subsequently traded by the owners who made the market.

The Early Years

The first open-end mutual fund was created by Edward Leffler, who previously sold securities. By 1929, there were 19 open-end funds holding a total of $140 million, which seems like considerable money for the time. However, at the same time, there were nearly 90 closed-end trusts, which held $3 billion in total assets.

The timing of the birth of these funds was not favorable, and the problems encountered by the funds in the Stock Market Crash of 1929 were compounded by managers leveraging the assets of the investors — a common practice when an investor feels that the market will only go upward and borrows money to multiply his or her gains. Notice that the lessons of the past are not always learned, as evidenced by financial companies such as Lehman Brothers in the present day still being caught out by over-leveraging the funds at their disposal.

The open-end funds fared better in the Stock Market Crash than the closed-end funds did. Managers of the closed-end funds were secretive and did not always disclose what shares were held. The managers could even value the shares at whatever price they chose, which led to dubious practices. In contrast, the open-end funds had a policy of declaring a net-asset value, as they permitted redemption upon demand, and this served to keep out the extremes of borrowing and other manipulations.

The Introduction of Regulation

As a consequence of the great Crash, Congress passed a succession of laws involving securities. In 1933, the Securities Act set rules for anyone who offered publicly traded securities, requiring that the company offering the securities register them with the Federal Trade Commission and produce a prospectus to describe the securities to potential investors.

This was followed in 1934 with the Securities Exchange Act, whose principal effect was to create the Securities and Exchange Commission (SEC), which enforced the federal laws affecting securities. This act later required further registration by parties involved in offering the securities.

Prior to these federal laws, there was little federal ruling enacted to protect investors, but some states designated laws that controlled the fund's operations. Bringing control to the federal government was a major step forward to avoid some of the problems that had been encountered before.

In 1936, the Revenue Act established a benefit for mutual funds that allowed ordinary companies to have a "pass-through" tax methodology, which means that the funds are not taxed on their profits in the way a normal company is taxed. Instead, the shareholders are taxed on the distributions, avoiding double taxation. One of the requirements imposed as a condition of this arrangement is that mutual funds must redeem the shares on demand, which benefits shareholders. Further regulation was specifically geared toward the mutual fund industry. In 1940, two acts were passed: the Investment Advisers Act and the Investment Company Act. The latter sought to regulate investment companies, which included closed-end funds, open-end funds, and investment trusts, and is the basis from which all regulation of mutual funds has proceeded. In contrast to the 1933 Securities Act, which mainly governed the openness with which business was conducted, the 1940 Act provided regulation and required specific duties.

The Investment Advisers Act imposes regulations and restrictions on the company that manages the mutual fund. In addition to being registered with the SEC, the fund must keep mandated records and act in the best interest of the shareholders to whom it has a fiduciary duty.

The result of these regulations is that the shareholder in a mutual fund can be assured that his or her interests are legally protected. Consequently, you will find that most of the recent financial scandals concern other types of funds, such as hedge funds, which do not have the restrictions imposed by these laws.

Boosts for the Mutual Fund

In addition to regulating mutual funds, laws have been passed over the years that have benefited and popularized mutual funds, particularly in the realm of retirement and savings accounts.

In 1974, the Employee Retirement Income Security Act (ERISA) was passed, creating the principle of an Individual Retirement Account (IRA), and the 401(k) retirement plan came into being with the Revenue Act of 1978. Both of these retirement savings plans draw heavily on mutual funds for their investment vehicles.

Public awareness of these opportunities increased in the last two decades, when mutual funds seemed to offer a better rate of return than putting money into savings accounts or Certificates of Deposit (CDs).

The Investment Companies

During the latter half of the 20th century, the mutual fund industry exploded with growth. In these last few decades, the well-known names of the financial industry came into existence and formed the companies with which we are now familiar: Vanguard®, Fidelity®, and Prudential are just some of the examples worth considering for an investment.

In 1975, John Bogle founded the Vanguard Group, which now comprises a large selection of different funds that are generally seen as the leaders in the business. These have a consistently low cost to the investor and are organized in a not-for-profit arrangement. Bogle himself is an advocate for index funds rather than actively managed funds, primarily because he believes that the additional cost is not worthwhile for the individual investor.

Fidelity's funds, another giant, have an enormous following and have created some of the stars of the mutual fund industry. Peter Lynch managed the Fidelity Magellan fund for years and increased the fund's holdings from $26 million to $14 billion in the period up to 1990. Some of this increase came from popularity, but a great deal came from the performance that he managed to rack up: nearly a 30 percent return per year.

The Mechanics

There is a diverse number of different investments that can be made by the manager, and the choice of these is affected by what the fund's aims are. The fund that suits you may not suit your neighbor, and what suits you this year may not suit you the next. It is important that you know the details of your funds and their components and that, once you have invested, you review your holding at least annually to see whether any changes should be made.

When you put money into a mutual fund, you become a shareholder in that fund, just as if you had bought shares in a company on the stock market. The fund will usually have stated objectives for its investment plan, which cover topics such as the type of shares or bonds that will be bought by the fund and how much risk the manager intends to take. Though you can get a general idea of the fund from this description, always research further to see what actual holdings the fund has and to determine whether they fit your objectives.

One of the best features of a mutual fund, compared with investing individually, is that a typical mutual fund controls a large amount of money. Consequently, the fund manager can buy stocks in several different companies for the much-vaunted diversification that most experts advise. Diversification ensures that any wrong stock pick will not have a marked effect on the value as a whole, even if that company should fail completely. The large number of companies represented in a typical fund means that the fund is not greatly affected when a financial catastrophe occurs at one of the companies, although a manager will likely know to sell the shares before they reach that stage.

The following particular terms will be heard often when people talk about mutual funds, and they can have a significant effect on the returns you see on your investment.

Costs

Naturally, there are costs associated with holding shares in a mutual fund. The fund must pay the manager and cover other expenses, and they all must have a regular fee for operating expenses. This covers the office costs, fund manager and administration salaries, and other assorted expenses. This tends to be expressed as a percentage charged per year. The charge can vary from a fraction of a percent — particularly for index mutual funds in which the fund has an investing program, which is almost automatic compared to other types — up to 1 or more percent for funds that require more management. This varies to some extent with the size of the fund, with the larger, more popular funds having lower expense ratios because of the total funds invested.

Be aware that many funds charge in other ways, and you should consider all costs and expenses you may incur when evaluating the fund. For instance, some funds, called "load funds," include a commission fee. The costs associated with mutual funds are not so simply summarized as whether they have a load and what the expense ratio is, though. There are other ways in which charges can be levied, and you will must learn to read a prospectus to fully grasp where your money may be going.

Underlying Assets

This will be covered in detail in a later chapter, but you must understand the underlying assets on which a particular fund is based to realistically determine the risk and reward basis of any fund you are considering investing in. While no one can predict the actual performance of a fund, you will want to have a feel for how risky a fund may be — particularly if it represents your retirement savings.

Many mutual funds invest in the stock market and thus take on the risks associated with that financial area. The stock market is known to beat the rate of inflation and other investments over the long-term and is a favored place for people who know that they do not need to have access to their money for many years. In the shorter-term, it is unreliable for money that may be needed for an emergency, as the stock market tends to go through cycles.

When you choose a mutual fund that has all or some of its investments in stocks, you will also select the size of the companies that the fund specializes in; what market sector it specializes in, such as energy or health; and whether the fund invests in the United States only, in another country's stocks, or in an international mix of stocks.

Funds may also invest in bonds, which are a debt instrument, as opposed to stocks, which represent ownership. You will find that most things you invest in fall into one of these categories.

To make clear the difference between stocks and bonds, consider the example of buying a house. A mortgage is debt, like a bond, and if you own part of a mortgage company or carry a note on a property, you have paid out money in return for a promise of repayment with interest, much like a bondholder. With the example of a mortgage, you have the security that your money is safe, as there is a contractual agreement that you can seize the house for its value in foreclosure proceedings to attempt to recover the money owed to you.

If, instead of lending money to someone else, you use your money to buy a house, you are taking ownership of an asset, and you may hope that the asset will increase in value so you can receive more money over time. This is the position you are in when you buy stocks. These two concepts, of debt represented by bonds or of ownership represented by stocks, may influence what fund you want to invest in.

Bonds come in various forms, though they all represent debt. The borrower may be the government — national, state, or local — like in Treasury Bonds. On the other hand, the borrower or issuer of the bonds may be a corporation, which usually means the interest rate is higher to compensate for increased risk, as they may not be considered as secure and reliable as the government.

Though bonds are considered safer than stocks because they represent money borrowed — which would be repaid first if the company were to file for bankruptcy — the price of bonds is likely to vary according to the rate of interest offered; therefore, you can experience capital gains or losses in the short term.

Consider a case in which the rate of interest on the bond is relatively and comparatively low. Investors would not want to buy the bonds at face value, as they could buy others of the same type at the same level of risk that would give them a better return. Consequently, the bonds would sell at less than face value or at a discount. This effectively increases the interest rate on the amount invested to match what can currently be obtained.

On the other hand, if the bonds were committed to a higher rate of interest, then they would cost more than their face value, and investors would pay more for them to get the increased revenue. Thus, market forces will cause bonds to vary in price.

The other variable affecting bond prices is how long it is before it is due to be repaid. For a short-term loan, the principal will be paid back soon, and the value of the bond will not vary much from the face value. In contrast, long-term bonds will be most affected by market interest-rate fluctuations.

You may also invest in an index fund if you prefer the lower administration costs and are content with the returns of the market as a whole. Furthermore, many managed funds do not beat the market consistently, which may give you more reason to settle for the index. In its simplest form, the index fund invests in all the companies that comprise the index. For example, the Vanguard 500 Index Fund is designed to match the performance of the Standard & Poor's 500 Index® by investing in all 500 of the companies that make up the index. This is called "passive management," as the investment decisions are virtually automatic. Some index funds will save the complication of holding so many companies by reducing variation and holding just a few companies in each market sector, which is usually an effective compromise.

Another fund in a class of its own is the money market fund, which often comes with the facility of a checkbook and can be used instead of the more traditional bank account for large sums. The underlying assets are high-yielding "financial instruments," which generally require a large investment that few individuals can afford. The money market fund offers convenient access to this sector of the market.

The following is an overview of the sorts of vehicles that a mutual fund can put your money into. For a detailed description of all the different shares, bonds, and other financial instruments that a mutual fund might invest in, see the later chapter on types of investments.

Regulation

What constitutes a mutual fund is defined by regulation. Discussion about the regulation of mutual funds occurs frequently throughout this book, as they are carefully controlled by legislation and monitored for their compliance. For instance, information about what you are entitled to receive as an investor in the fund and the form of that information is consistently defined, which is in contrast to other investments, such as hedge funds, which have not been so carefully scrutinized in the past. Given the financial crisis and the scandal about Bernie Madoff's investment practices, this situation may change, but legislation for mutual funds will likely remain the same.

Mutual funds are heavily regulated compared to many other investments you may be considering. Any legitimate mutual fund must endure considerable scrutiny before beginning to offer shares, and that scrutiny is ongoing, with close examination at its operations to ensure that investors are adequately protected. However, that does not mean that you cannot lose money with a mutual fund; just as with any other investment, if you or the fund manager chooses unwisely, you are vulnerable to losing money, and mutual funds will charge you for management even if you do lose, which will hurt you even more. You have many choices in what type of mutual fund to invest your money in, and for most people, several varieties with different levels of risks are the best options.

The SEC is the body responsible for looking after your interests and controlling the operations of mutual fund companies. You have likely heard of the SEC in connection with many financial matters, as they are one of the main regulating boards. Toward the end of 2008, the SEC became especially well-known because of the major financial issues that arose. To be fair, the SEC regulates to the extent that it is able to, and when financial investment companies take excessive and failed risks, the fault lies with the companies' management.

Despite this, the SEC took an active role in trying to relieve the credit crisis, working with the Federal Reserve, the Department of the Treasury, and other regulating bodies to resolve the problems caused for investors. Though the SEC is an effective regulating body, it is sometimes called in only when problems start to appear — and it has to pick up the pieces.

Mutual funds do not tend to become involved with riskier investments like subprime mortgages, thus a more likely problem they face is a general decline in value when the stock market goes through a downward cycle. It is possible to invest in mutual funds that have basis in derivatives, which is an investment vehicle that multiplies gains and losses beyond the invested amount, and these are often riskier. But most are not based in derivatives, and you will learn how to determine the make-up of each fund and hence assess your own risk.

Setting up a mutual fund includes a detailed review by the Commission, and the founders of the fund cannot ask for investment until it has completed this to the satisfaction of the SEC. The chief form is called the N-1A, which registers the mutual fund as a company and registers its shares under the governing Acts. In addition, to establish the legitimate structure for the fund, the creators must fill out Form ADV, which is an application for registration as an investment advisor that names the person responsible for controlling the investment practices. Some states also have additional regulations that must be complied with, thus setting up a mutual fund is not quite as easy or as casual as forming an investment club.

The SEC will examine the mutual fund's prospectus for full compliance with its extensive requirements. The prospectus will be discussed in a later chapter but, for now, understand that its contents are regulated and required, and that these provisions are intended to safeguard the interests of the mutual fund investors.

CHAPTER 2

Types of Mutual Funds

Open-End Funds

Open-end funds are the most commonly encountered type. This term means that the fund will sell you shares at any time without undue restrictions; the fund is "open" to new investment. If many people decide they want to put their money into an open-end fund, the fund manager must decide what to do with the new money — whether to increase the fund's holdings in the existing securities, buy into new securities, or a do combination of these.

If a fund is popular, then the total amount of money invested will increase, which may help keep down management costs because a percentage of investments allow the fund to employ a more talented manager at a higher salary — without increasing the cost to the investors.

Closed-End Funds

On the other hand, closed-end funds are restricted and vary in several ways from open-end funds. Here, the mutual fund company decides when the fund is established how many shares the fund will have. Much like having shares in a company such as General Electric (GE®), these mutual funds are traded through brokers similarly. Because there are a fixed number of shares, you must find someone who wants to sell shares in order to buy a stake in this mutual fund. With the need of a broker, you will be charged a commission for buying or selling.

While it is easy to value a share in an open-end fund — all you need to do is check the price and number of securities that are held — the value of a share in a closed-end fund depends on what current investors think they are worth. This means that they may trade more cheaply or expensively than the underlying security holdings, and the price will reflect what the investors believe the future value will be. Unless you have great confidence in the fund's potential, try to purchase a closed-end fund at a discount to have some inherent value built in.

Closed-end funds do not have their values listed in the mutual fund tables that appear in many newspapers. Instead, you must look in the tables of prices for stocks, specifically under the stock exchange where they are traded.

CASE STUDY: DOUGLAS G. OBER.

Douglas G. Ober is the Chairman and Chief Executive Officer of two closed-end funds, The Adams Express Company and Petroleum & Resources Corporation, with combined assets of more than $2 billion. Both funds have been investment companies traded on the New York Stock Exchange (NYSE®) since 1929, with Adams Express previously involved in a nationwide delivery business. Ober joined the firms in 1980 as a research analyst, became a member of the portfolio management team in 1986, and was elected chairman of the companies in 1991.

Prior to his employment at Adams Express and Petroleum & Resources, Ober was employed at the First National Bank of Maryland for eight years in commercial lending. Previous employment, from 1968 until 1971, was with the U.S. Naval Air Test Center as a Test Project Engineer.

Ober received his Bachelor of Science degree in engineering from Princeton University, a master's degree in finance from Loyola College in Baltimore, Maryland, and a certificate from the Advanced Management Program of the Wharton School of the University of Pennsylvania. He is also a graduate of the U.S. Naval Test Pilot School.

A Chartered Financial Analyst, Ober is a member of the Baltimore Security Analysts Society and the New York Society of Security Analysts, and is a past representative of closed-end funds on the Board of Governors of the Investment Company Institute. He is currently a member of the Executive Committee of the Closed-End Fund Association.

Questions asked by:

Adams Express Company
www.adamsexpress.com
410-752-5900
800-638-2479

Answers provided by:

Petroleum & Resources Corporation
www.peteres.com
410-752-5900
800-638-2479

CASE STUDY: DOUGLAS G. OBER.

How did you get into the field of closed-end funds?

After eight years as a commercial banker and the comple-
tion of a master's degree in finance, I sought opportunities in equity research. Adams Express, having moved
to Baltimore just four years earlier from New York, was
seeking a technology analyst and felt that my undergradu-
ate degree in engineering, along with the finance degree
and experience in credit analysis, would be a good fit.

**As Chairman and CEO of Adams Express and Petroleum & Resources, what do
you see as your primary function when selecting investments?**

In my position, I am the senior member of the portfolio management teams of
both funds. Our research staff brings up ideas for inclusion in the portfolios,
which we then evaluate for their appropriateness in the funds. I bring 28 years
of market experience to the table and seek out overlooked strengths and weak-
nesses in new investment ideas. As the chief economist of the firm, I also look
at ideas from a macroeconomic perspective, seeing if they will perform well
during the next phase of the economic cycle. I consider myself the principal
representative of our shareholders in this process as well. I want to ensure that
we make investment decisions that are in the very best interests of our shareholders over the long-term.

**Given the current state of the financial markets, have you changed the way that
you select any investments, or is your existing strategy already coping well?**

We have consistently devoted a good portion of our analysis to the balance
sheets and cash flows of companies. If anything, we devote more time to that
now. Our funds, being closed-end, take a longer view of the market and do not
turn over the portfolios nearly as much as mutual funds (ADX 5-year average
turnover — 13.2 percent, PEO — 11.6 percent). As a consequence, balance-
sheet strength takes on greater importance, as it has during this credit crisis.

What do you like and dislike about closed-end funds?

The structure of a closed-end fund enables the portfolio manager to consider a
universe of stocks that an open-end (mutual) fund manager cannot. Less liquid
securities, 144(a) issues, and convertible securities have all been used by the
funds, as there is no risk of fund redemptions and forced liquidation of positions — especially during bear markets like today's.

CASE STUDY: DOUGLAS G. OBER.

Closed-end funds are also permitted to use leverage, which has caused some difficulty in the recent frozen markets. During more favorable periods, leverage can significantly increase the returns available to common shareholders.

Another attractive aspect of closed-end funds, particularly ones that are internally managed like ours, is their stability. Management turnover is infrequent; the portfolio doesn't change dramatically from quarter to quarter, so shareholders have some idea of what they are invested in; and mergers or acquisitions are rare, so funds don't disappear.

On the other hand, closed-end funds are largely ignored by the industry's largest trade group and the media. The principal subject matter of articles about the funds is their discount, the difference between the market price of the shares, and their net asset value. We like to point out the opportunities created by discounts — investing 85 cents and getting a dollar's worth of return, and trading around the discount — buying when it's wide and selling when it narrows. The media tends to focus on the existence of a discount: Why don't the shares trade at net asset value like an open-end fund; what is management doing to narrow or eliminate the discount? Shareholders have the right to get net asset value for their shares. My response is to ask how many shareholders purchased their shares at net asset value; usually, the answer is only those who bought an IPO, and so why would they expect to be able to sell them at net asset value?

A number of closed-end funds formed a trade group several years ago, primarily to educate investors on the benefits of closed-end funds and respond to media inquiries. We have had some success, as the investing public is more aware of this class of investment, but it is frustrating to have to constantly explain the differences between closed-end and mutual funds.

What personal qualities do you think help you succeed in your role today?

I am a relatively risk-averse individual, which has been important in the past 18 months in stock selection. I believe my personal integrity is without question and, therefore, I have the trust of our staff, board of directors, and, importantly, our shareholders. I have assembled a staff that operates exceedingly well as a team, with little conflict but a willingness to express different views. Strong leadership is critical in today's environment. I believe I bring a quiet strength to our organization that is highly valued.

CASE STUDY: DOUGLAS G. OBER.

What is the biggest success you have had concerning closed-end funds?

As the former President and a current Executive Committee member of the Closed-End Fund Association, I have represented our industry in the media, in front of investors, and to Wall Street. The industry has gained considerable respect in all these arenas, and I have been a contributor to that. We are no longer considered stepchildren of the mutual fund industry or an investment oddity. There is a place in investment portfolios today for closed-end funds that almost did not exist 15 years ago.

What is the biggest challenge that you have had to face?

When I took over management of the companies, we had a staff that did not work well together, with several fiefdoms existing and little sharing of ideas or information among the research staff. Forming a cohesive team of personnel with the goals of providing the best returns possible to shareholders and an enjoyable place to work was a difficult task. Several individuals were fired and some permitted to retire early, all while maintaining strong internal controls and a solid investment portfolio.

What advice would you give to potential investors, particularly in the face of the economic crisis, and how would this vary depending on their age?

On a regular basis, at least once a year, evaluate your needs and desires as they relate to income, capital appreciation, and risk. With the huge reduction in the past year in assets set aside for retirement, everyone needs to reconsider their savings goals and how they are going to attain them. Those with a long period of time until retirement should rely primarily on equities to build their savings, with some portion thereof in more aggressive growth stocks. Those with a shorter time frame should consider a blend of somewhat less risky equities and fixed income securities, with at least a 50 percent weighting in equities, given life expectancies at this time.

Retirees should also maintain some equity exposure, as long as an appropriate level of income is generated by their investment portfolio. With the single exception of the Great Depression, equities have done very well following periods of economic slowdown. Selling off one's entire equity portfolio after a major retrenchment in the stock market would, I believe, be a great mistake.

Net Asset Value

As mentioned above, it is easy to value the shares of an open-end fund. You can find out the number of shares that have been sold in the fund and the value of the securities that the fund holds. Each mutual fund share is worth the total security value divided by the number of shares, called the net asset value (NAV) of the share.

Because the NAV depends on the values of the securities held by the fund, it will vary daily. When you invest in mutual funds, it is best not to check the value too often, as fluctuation is normal; investment is for the long-term, and you rarely need to worry about daily price movements.

For a closed-end fund, the NAV will depend on the marketplace and the opinion of buyers and sellers in the fund. There will be an underlying value that can be calculated, but this will only give you a guide to the market price.

No-Load Funds

Many mutual funds are now no-load funds, which means they do not charge you a commission to buy them — you must only pay the NAV for the number of shares you purchase. As a rule, you purchase shares directly from the mutual fund, which means there are no brokers or salespeople who demand a commission.

However, as pointed out in the chapter on costs and fees, be warned that some mutual fund companies are becoming more aggressive with obtaining more money from you. Some apparently no-load funds may charge backend loads, which are sales charges paid when you leave the fund rather than when you buy into it. The difference between backend loads and redemption fees, both of which are incurred when you leave the fund, is that loads are calculated on the amount you invested, while redemption fees are calculated from the value of your fund assets and may even be on a sliding scale, reducing over time to discourage those who wish to frequently trade their funds.

Load Funds

Commission-free or no-load funds used to be the exception. The load fund is sold to an investor at net asset value plus a sales commission, otherwise known as a load. Most of these are handled by brokers and other selling organizations, and the commission fees may be as much as 8 percent of the total price. This means that for every $100 you invest, only $92 goes into buying securities in the fund.

This is a significant handicap at the start of your investment, and the fund must perform excellently for a year or more before you even show a gain on the money you paid. You may wonder why anyone would buy a load fund when no-load funds are available. This may be because they feel that the fund manager is exceptional at his job and will produce better returns than the other funds can; however, many studies have shown that regardless of whether you are charged a load, the funds do not necessarily perform much differently.

Tax-Free Funds

As your money is invested in different securities, you will find that you have a potential tax liability on any gains you make. The return that you get from a mutual fund can come in various ways.

You may get capital gains, which are usually sent out once or twice a year. These come from the manager selling stock or securities during the year at a higher price than he or she bought them and are usually issued net — that is, after the allowable expenses are deducted.

You will also qualify for any dividend distributions. Some stocks and bonds issue dividends, and you are entitled to your share of them. Both capital gains and dividends can be re-invested in the mutual fund to buy more shares in the fund for you, and if you do not need the money, this is a good way to rapidly increase your holding and generate wealth. This is similar to compounding interest in an interest-paying bank savings account.

Of course, these income sources may be liable for taxation. You can have the mutual funds held in a retirement account, which will change the tax treatment — often deferring the tax to a later time — but otherwise, you may find that you have a tax bill. If you prefer to avoid this situation, consider investing in tax-free funds, which reduce or eliminate this problem.

Tax-free funds usually have a lower earnings expectation, which compensates to some degree for the elimination of taxes. However, for this reason, you would likely not want to hold tax-free funds in a retirement account, in which you are not required to pay the tax right away. If you are in a higher tax bracket, a tax-free fund may work out better for you.

It is not just a case of the fund manager deciding whether the fund will make taxable payments; it is the choices that he or she makes in accordance with the fund's plan that decide what tax is due. For instance, if the fund invests in government-issued Treasury bonds, the dividends are considered free of state taxes, although they do have a federal tax liability. Better yet, the dividends of a municipal bond fund, which invest in local government and state bonds, are free of federal tax, and if you live in the same state as the originating state of the bonds, the dividends are also state tax-free.

These options are only available with money market or bond funds, as they are able to invest in the tax-friendly bonds mentioned above. If you have a mutual fund that invests in stocks, you will be liable for taxes on any distributions if the fund is held outside a retirement account. The way the fund is managed will make a difference on when and how you pay the taxes. For example, a manager that buys and holds stocks for a long period rather than constantly trading will have an effect because long-term capital gains have a lower tax rate than short-term.

World Fund

A world fund is a mutual fund that invests in securities from several different countries and may have up to 75 percent of the capital invested in the United States. It is better regarded as a mutual fund, which has the capability of diversifying into the best investment ideas from other countries, as well as having a core U.S. holding.

In a world fund, the manager has the opportunity to look around internationally for the best investment opportunities rather than be limited to a specific country. With an experienced manager, this type of fund can hedge against currency fluctuations and benefit from emerging markets and growth in other countries.

Some regard the world fund an ideal combination of base investment in America with retained flexibility, and the limited overseas investment means that the fund is not heavily exposed to currency fluctuations.

Global Fund

The term "global fund" may apply to a mutual fund, in which case it is similar to a world fund, but the term may equally well refer to an exchange-traded fund (ETF), which means that the manager of the fund can invest in companies and other financial instruments from anywhere in the world, providing the utmost flexibility for diversification and protection against currency fluctuations.

Depending on the manager's stated objectives, the global fund includes investments in companies in the United States, and the manager is free to diversify into foreign opportunities to hedge against currency changes and inflation.

International Fund

In contrast to the global fund, an international fund usually refers to a fund that invests in companies anywhere outside the investor's country. In other words, an international fund only invests in places that the investor considers foreign. This allows an investor more control over the composition of his or her portfolio and the proportion of foreign investments that it contains.

As it only refers to the location of the companies or other financial securities in which the fund invests, this term can be applied not only to mutual funds, but also to ETFs and hedge funds.

Foreign Fund

This is another name for the international fund. Again, the distinction from a global fund is that it specifically excludes investments in the investor's home country. This provides a convenient way for investors to have access to markets outside their domicile, which, if they were to invest in them as an individual, might require an investor to set up separate brokerage accounts.

The statement of objective for the fund should provide more detail on the types of overseas investments the manager is seeking. It can, for instance, specify whether the fund will concentrate on developed or developing countries, and the types of market sector that the manager is open to investing in.

Regional Fund

A regional fund is a more specific type of international or foreign fund and is widely accepted to be a fund that confines itself to a particular geographical area, such as Europe or the Middle East.

It will often own a diversified portfolio in the region, but it is not limited to this. Depending on the fund's objectives, it may specialize not only in an area of the world, but also in a market sector, such as energy.

This can be an effective investment tool for the small investor, as it is unlikely that he or she would otherwise have easy access to invest in many companies in a region. It also guarantees exposure to the particular region of the world that the investor is interested in, in contrast to the world or global fund, in which the manager decides on the exposure to different regions.

Emerging Market Fund

The emerging market fund can be a mutual or exchange-traded fund, and most of its investment will be made in one or more developing countries. This may be an even more specific selection than the regional fund and is often considered riskier than the average — but with the promise of great returns.

The emerging market could be somewhere like Hong Kong, China, or Singapore. It is possible to buy emerging market funds, which are called diversified emerging markets, which gives the manager flexibility to see which area of the globe he or she feels will provide the best gains.

The risk level for an emerging market fund will vary widely depending on the companies in which the fund invests. For instance, the fund may choose to invest only in established large companies, which tend to be less risky than start-up companies.

Single-Country Fund

Sometimes associated with the emerging market funds, the single-country fund comprises stocks and financial instruments based in one country. This type of fund can have high volatility and can also achieve a good performance, though it is subject to the changing exchange rate with the chosen country, which may serve to amplify the gains or losses.

The mutual fund prospectus will explain the investment strategy and, if it is a single-country strategy, the fund must abide by this statement. This limits the manager in what he or she can do if the chosen country suffers an economic downturn. Depending on the size of the market in the country selected, there may also be liquidity problems when the fund managers change their investments. You may also see this type of fund referred to as a "country fund."

Sector Fund

Sector funds confine themselves to investing in a particular sector of the economy, concentrating on just one industry, such as energy or health care. The idea is to give mutual fund investors the opportunity to concentrate on a sector that they think is strong and will yield good growth.

Choosing to invest in a sector fund is, of course, the antithesis of the much-vaunted diversification. Because mutual funds are frequently selected for a portfolio because of their built-in diversification, the reasons for investing in a sector fund must be evaluated differently from the general intent to invest in a mutual fund.

Diversification is a matter of perception, however. If an investor were inclined to put money in one or two health care stocks, investing in a sector fund that specialized in health care would give much better diversification within that market segment.

There is a hidden danger in expecting a sector fund to get the profits you anticipate that segment of the market will enjoy. For example, you may believe that biotechnology is a growth area and be interested in a sector fund that invests in biotech, but what the fund manager understands by this may be quite different from what you intended. If you look at biotech sector funds, you will find a variety of companies with widely varying products: Some will be concentrated on the world of genomics; others may be drug manufacturers; and still others will focus more heavily on research — perhaps in a specialized field, such as cancer.

While this is an example of diversification, it may also not be the best play to accord with your expectations of growth in the biotech sector. If you have specific knowledge or information of a market sector, you may find that buying a single stock will be more satisfactory.

Multi-Advisor Fund

This term refers to a style of fund management. It appears most commonly in the hedge fund market, although they can also be applied to mutual funds. Here, the fund is managed by several people, each with their own expertise; for instance, one of the managers may specialize in emerging markets.

Depending on the management structure in the fund management company, advisers will not typically be fully autonomous but will present their knowledge and recommendation for discussion to the other managers. With their superior knowledge, they will usually expect to gain the approval of the others, but as joint managers, the full team will want to be involved in any investment decision. Therefore, a multi-advisor fund is stronger than a single advisor's recommendation.

A multi-advisor fund often has an international focus, with an advisor specializing in Middle Eastern energy stocks, for example, and another advisor perhaps responsible for Asian technology. Considering the complexity of the modern financial markets, it is increasingly necessary for advisors to specialize, and a multi-advisor fund is a good solution to this challenge.

Sub-Advised Fund

In contrast to the multi-advisor fund, the sub-advised fund is actually managed out-of-house — that is, there are no advisors on the investments working at the mutual fund company. Instead, the fund company employs another management team or company to direct the investments.

This may occur for a variety of reasons, but your main concern in considering a sub-advised fund is the fee structure, as both the fund company and the management company receive payment for their work.

Incubated Fund

You may not have heard of an incubated fund, as it is not offered to the public. This term refers to a fund privately sold when it is first created, typically to employees and family members. It is used by fund managers to test their strategies before opening the fund to the public and submitting to regulation. Managers may try different styles of investing to see which work best, commonly called a "limited distribution" fund.

If the returns on the fund are found to be positive, then the fund will potentially be made available to the public; otherwise, it will be liquidated and forgotten. Depending on the investing strategy and goals of the manager, the fund can go on to become a mutual fund, hedge fund, or other fund variety.

Incubated funds have been criticized because the lack of regulation when trying out strategies can affect the results. This means that the returns may not be so easily achievable if the fund is transformed into a full-fledged mutual fund. It is not always clear when looking at a mutual fund whether the fund has developed in this way, as managers will often try to hide these origins.

Fund of Funds

As suggested by the name, a fund of funds is a mutual fund that invests in other mutual funds. This allows you to have broad diversification with just one investment, but it does come with the disadvantage that you are paying management fees to the fund of fund manager — in addition to the fees for the funds that are invested in. Because of this structured management arrangement, these are sometimes called multi-management funds.

Funds of funds did not always show expenses that reflected the underlying expenses — the fund manager formerly would indicate his or her expenses and consider the subordinate funds' expenses not relevant. However, the SEC started requiring all expenses to be disclosed starting in January 2007, so you should not run into this problem.

Master Fund

A master fund is a fund that invests in other underlying investments, which are operated by professional managers. As such, the type of fund depends on what the underlying funds seek to achieve, so it may be a mutual fund, but could equally well be a hedge fund.

A master fund often comes in the form of a fund of funds but could also be a feeder fund, buying into another fund.

Feeder Fund

A feeder fund manages its investment through other funds. Though similar to a fund of funds, these use a fund manager, who is responsible for managing the underlying investments. The public can only invest through the feeder fund, which in turn invests in the underlying funds.

This arrangement is sometimes used for its potential tax advantage; for instance, a feeder fund may invest in an offshore master fund. If you are interested in pursuing this idea, seek the advice of a tax professional.

Targeted-Distribution Fund

The targeted-distribution fund is a type of mutual fund. As the name implies, the manager concentrates on the distributions paid out to the shareholders. The distributions may come from capital gains and from income such as dividends. These types of funds are suitable to replace a steady income, such as those you would need in retirement, and are also known as open-end managed-payout funds.

Targeted-distribution funds can be operated in various manners. Some funds will specify the amount that they pay each month, while others vary the amount depending on the portfolio performance. The overall performance of the fund will determine whether the initial investment is depleted in making the regular payments. It is important to note that this fund is not like an annuity in that there is no guarantee the payments will be maintained. The fund's viability will depend on the level of payout, the performance of the portfolio, and the manager's skill.

Life-Cycle Fund

A life-cycle fund is a special category of mutual fund in which the balance of the asset allocation is adjusted during the fund's life, usually from higher to lower risk; this is primarily designed for retirement planning so that the balance of the investment becomes safer as retirement approaches. They are a fairly recent invention and are marketed as a hands-off way for individuals to invest in their retirement.

If you have enough interest in investing to read this book, however, a life-cycle fund is likely not for you. It appeals to the investor who wants to lock away his or her funds and not look at them again until they are needed. With the information in this book, you are better equipped to take care of your own risk management and adjust as you see necessary as retirement approaches.

Another problem cited for life-cycle funds is that they must take a certain view of the level of risk you should have at a set number of years from retirement. This one-size-fits-all approach may not be suitable for you, as everyone's risk tolerance is different and depends on many factors, including upbringing and financial well-being.

Life-cycle funds are also referred to as "age-based funds," "target-date funds," and "target risk funds." Although life-cycle funds used to be limited to mutual funds, you are now able to find some life-cycle exchange-traded funds in the market.

Target-Date Fund

A target-date fund is a life-cycle fund that assumes a model asset allocation based on the number of years before your retirement. Many people are familiar with the concept of shifting funds into safer investments as you approach the time when you need to withdraw them, and this is most often expressed as a percentage of stocks compared with a percentage of bonds in your holdings.

The target-date variety are funds of funds — that is, they hold several different mutual funds in their portfolio, and the percentage of each is adjusted as time passes. The farther away the target date is, the riskier the investments. As the date approaches, the portfolio is adjusted into less risky mutual funds; after the target date, the funds are mostly in fixed-income investments.

Arguably, you are incurring more expenses by selecting a target-date fund because you will be paying the expenses on the mutual funds held as well as additional expenses for management of the target-date fund. A target-date fund tends to contain only funds from the same fund company, and you could buy these in the same proportion outside the target-date fund and save the additional management costs.

These funds are usually classified in terms of whether they are considered high, medium, or low-risk funds for the target date selected, and the date tends to be part of the name of the fund. However, different fund companies have different ideas of the amount of risk that is acceptable, and you will find different proportions between equities and fixed-income applications with funds that are intended for the same retirement date.

If the retirement date is 25 or more years away, the target date fund will hold about 90 percent of your investment in stock mutual funds, with the rest in bond funds and cash. As a guide, you should expect that the proportions will shift to about 50 percent stocks and 50 percent bonds and cash by the time the target date is reached. The prospectus for the target date fund will explain the target allocations that the fund's managers believe are appropriate.

These funds are also intended to reflect the correct mix of equity and fixed income for your investments according to the funds' managers, which means that if you hold any funds outside the target-date fund, you are upsetting that proportion. The retirement target-date fund is intended to be the only fund you should ever need. If you hold other funds in addition — and simple diversification suggests that you should — then you should continue to make regular adjustments to the proportions of the different types and risks in these funds. This detracts from the usefulness of the automatic adjustment in the target-date fund.

Target Risk Fund

The target risk fund is another type of fund of funds, as with the life-cycle funds. In this case, the fund manager does not adjust the balance over time but is committed to maintaining the overall risk exposure of the fund by changing the funds invested in when necessary. The target risk fund is also known as an active life-cycle fund, as you are required to be active and move your investment to a more conservative target risk fund as your retirement approaches.

You can generally find three different levels of risk — low risk (conservative), moderate risk, and high risk (aggressive). This gives a relative measure of the risk but is best used when comparing funds from the same fund family, as opinions may differ among different companies.

Again, this type of fund seems to be designed for the investor who does not wish to take much interest in his holdings, but rather wants a manager to control them. The disadvantage is that the manager of the target risk fund adds another layer of expenses to your investment. Over a period of time, such additional costs can mean a large difference in return.

Index Fund

An index fund is a type of mutual fund that tries to track or match a market index, such as the Dow Jones Wilshire 500, which reflects the stock market. This type of fund has a lower expense ratio, as the investments made do not require as much management expertise. If you own one of these funds, you would expect it to follow the general market — which, on average, does well.

Though a well-run mutual fund may consistently beat the market, a significant number do not, which provides an argument for investors who think an index fund may be the safest way of ensuring future returns.

These funds do have the advantage of a lower portfolio turnover, which means that your taxes on capital gains are lower while you hold the fund. The actual investments held can be a selection of all the stocks in the index or, sometimes, representative stocks are held to simplify the portfolio. In either case, you achieve broad market coverage and low expenses. This type of investing is sometimes called "passive investing."

Tracker Fund

A tracker fund is the same as an index fund, as the fund invests to try to emulate movement of the index. In its simplest form, this might mean buying all the shares that comprise the index, or a representative section of them. One of the advantages of this type of fund is that the costs tend to be low because the investment choices are automatic.

While unexciting, such a fund may not be a bad choice when you consider that the majority of mutual funds fail to beat the index of the market they invest in.

Enhanced Index Fund

Not to be confused with the regular index fund, an enhanced index fund tracks with a stock market index with enhancements. The enhancements generally include using leverage to try to beat the index.

Often, the index used is the S&P 500, and enhanced index funds are actively managed to beat the return of the index. This runs counter to the idea of the ordinary index fund, in which the reduced turnover and lower expenses help make the returns more effective. However, advocates of the enhanced index fund would argue that the increased returns more than cover the additional costs.

Equity Fund

An equity fund is a general term for a fund that invests in stocks or other security that represents an ownership. Within this general category are many types of stocks, and many of them are detailed here.

The term "equity fund" distinguishes this type of mutual fund from bond funds, which are based on debt rather than ownership.

Bond Fund

Bond funds come in many forms, but the common factor is that they invest in bonds. The type of bond may be treasury, corporate, or municipal, and the time until maturity of the bonds is another factor in selection of the fund.

Short-term bonds are less likely to vary much with change in interest rate, whereas the longer-term bonds are subject to fluctuations. Bond funds tend to concentrate on a particular type of bond, and you can find out more by studying the objectives in the prospectus.

Value Fund

A value fund is a mutual fund that specializes in investing in undervalued stocks and shares. The assumption is that if the stock is truly undervalued, then it will, at some stage, increase in price to a greater extent than the general market growth.

The assessment of the value of the share is made using fundamental analysis, which considers overall topics such as price-earnings ratio, capitalization, and earnings growth. The value may be depressed because of investors' sentiment or a bad quarterly report.

Value funds tend to be safe and will often own shares that yield dividends as well as capital appreciation. In this way, they contrast with the growth fund mutual fund, which focuses on capital growth.

Growth Fund

With a growth fund, focus is directed to capital appreciation, which comes from holding investments in what are called "growth stocks." The difference from value funds is that growth funds do not tend to worry much about dividends, as the fund manager will look particularly at companies with increasing earnings or market share with the goal of making large capital gains.

These types of companies tend to reinvest their earnings into expansion or research. As they are in the expansion phase of company growth, they may be volatile, and it may be some time before you realize the expected value.

Money Market Fund

It has long been thought that a money market fund is as good as cash. The money market fund is a type of mutual fund, not to be confused with a money market account, which is a deposit account at a bank.

The money market fund is required by law to invest in the low-risk securities, but the actual investments can take various forms — and with the financial crisis of 2008, the stability of money market funds was called into question.

Money market funds that invest solely in Treasury bills are available, but with different maturity dates. These funds do not yield a good return because the Treasury yields are low; after expenses, they pay well under 1 percent at the time of this publication. If the Treasury interest rates are further reduced, the fund managers may be forced to reduce their expenses to maintain the value of the fund.

However, the Treasury-based funds are the lowest risk type of money market fund. By convention, the next lowest risk are the government-only funds, which deal with debt from government agencies. These have holdings that may now be considered less certain, including Lehman Brothers® and Morgan Stanley. The government connection is that these agreements are secured by government-backed mortgage debt, which means the fund would get the collateral in case of default.

With a higher yield, the final class of money market funds are called general money funds, which invest in commercial paper and other low-risk securities.

What all these funds have in common is that they should be able to pay investors back at least $1 for every $1 invested; if the net asset value drops below $1, then the fund is said to "break the buck." This is the ultimate failing for a money market fund, and if the fund is from a large investment company, it is likely the money will be found from elsewhere to maintain the fund's reputation.

The present financial crisis has caused some questioning of this practice. Only one money market fund broke the buck from the time the concept was created in 1971 until the middle of September 2008. Then the Lehman Brothers filed for bankruptcy on September 15, 2008, and two money market funds "broke the buck" due to their holdings with Lehman.

The SEC instigated a temporary guarantee program in conjunction with the Treasury Department and is stepping in to install new safeguards for the long-term. It is likely that any major failing of a money market fund would cause further turmoil in the financial markets.

CHAPTER 3

What Other Fund Investments Are Available?

While the purpose of this book is to consider and explain all aspects of mutual funds, there are several other types of funds you can invest in, and you may consider them as alternatives or additions to a mutual fund-based portfolio. The following explains the various other funds and their differences from mutual funds.

Exchange-Traded Funds (ETFs)

An exchange-traded fund is similar to a mutual index fund that tracks an index. It gets its name from the fact that the fund is traded all day long on the major stock market exchanges, just like any ordinary stock. This is a fundamental difference from a mutual fund, which does not trade during the day. The price an ETF trades at is about the same as the net asset value of the underlying assets — the stocks and shares that comprise the ETF.

The fact that ETFs trade during the day allows an investor to know the price he or she is paying straight away, in contrast to a mutual fund, which is only valued at the end of day. The price for a mutual fund tends to be based on the closing prices for the underlying stocks.

ETFs were introduced in 1993 in the U.S. markets and were developed in Europe in 1999. They are rarely available for the individual investor to buy directly from the fund manager but are traded in large blocks of tens of thousands of ETF shares by large institutional investors, who may assume the role of market makers for individual investors to take part in the fund. As recently as 2008, the SEC authorized ETFs to go beyond their traditional role as an index fund by becoming actively managed.

The actual legal form of an ETF may be an open-end management investment company, similar to a mutual fund, or a unit investment trust. In either case, the regulations require that a new ETF receives permission from the SEC for relief from the rules of the Investment Company Act of 1940, which would otherwise prohibit the structure of the ETF. In 2008, the SEC proposed new rule changes to allow an ETF to be formed without claiming the exemption, defined as a registered open-end management investment company.

The purpose of an ETF is to provide an investor with an easy means to purchase a diversified selection of shares with low costs. It has all the attributes of an ordinary share in that it can be sold short, can have all options associated with it, and can be bought and sold with limit orders to ensure that trading only takes place within certain acceptable price ranges.

Because of their flexibility, it is also possible to purchase ETFs that vary from the concept of a pure index fund. For instance, some ETFs, also known as leveraged ETFs, use derivative investments to multiply the returns, or sometimes invert them. In other words, the gain in an index value may be multiplied by a factor of two in a particular ETF, or a loss in the index may result in an equivalent gain in an ETF designed to profit that way.

As mentioned above, ETFs are still being developed, and their scope is increasing. They can be used by long-term investors and by short-term traders because of their system of trading on the stock market; consequently, they can be a useful vehicle to complement your mutual fund portfolio.

Hedge Funds

With the Bernie Madoff case and other well-publicized instances, hedge funds have recently been considered dubious investments. As made evident by the name, it was not always intended to be this way. Provided that steps are taken to ensure that the hedge fund is properly run and meets your objectives, investment in a hedge fund can still have some advantages.

While you may have thought of this as a modern phenomenon, the first hedge fund was actually created in 1949 with the purpose of reducing danger, or to "hedge" against risk. To accomplish this, a hedge fund manager can access many different trading strategies — notably, short selling — to profit from a falling market. Various types of leveraging strategy are also used, including borrowing money over and above the investors' initial positions.

Because hedge funds are considered a sophisticated tool, investment in them is limited to people who are considered sophisticated in financial matters, which is judged primarily by the investor's wealth. Today, hedge funds are viewed more frequently as a way to increase returns at a higher risk, rather than a hedge against market fluctuations.

The manager of a hedge fund will receive a performance fee, which encourages him or her to try to maximize returns. This can be an good concept to ensure the manager's dedication but can also lead to taking more risks with other people's money. Astonishingly, compared with the one or two percent fees charged by mutual fund managers, a hedge fund may typically charge a 2 percent management fee plus a performance fee of 20 percent or more of the fund's profits.

Advocates of hedge funds will point out that this is an acceptable level of remuneration in return for a skilled manager handling your funds and, if you choose wisely, it can be a rewarding investment in your portfolio. The ability of the manager to use all the financial instruments at his disposal allows the best to shine even in bad conditions, such as 2008/2009, when some hedge funds were possibly the best-performing investments.

It is important to understand that hedge funds are meant for sophisticated investors and that investment restriction exists for a reason. Unlike mutual funds, there are not many regulations in place to control the actions of a hedge fund manager and, consequently, you must perform your own analysis to have confidence that you are directing your assets into the best place. Higher returns are associated with high risk, and a fund that performs well one year may be lackluster the next.

Exchange Fund

Not to be confused with exchange-traded funds, an exchange fund is a particular process allowed for an investor to delay paying capital gains tax. This method was introduced in 1999 to enable large holders of a single stock to diversify their investment without having to find money for the capital gains.

This fund is also sometimes called a "swap fund," and it allows the large stock holder to exchange his holding for a selection of other stocks. Because it does not directly involve the sale of the stocks, there is no taxable event that would cause capital gains tax to be payable.

It is important to note that capital gains will still be due when the holding is sold, and gains will be based on the initial purchase price of the original stocks. Thus, the investor does not escape from his or her tax liability.

CHAPTER 4

Underlying Investments in a Fund

Every mutual fund comprises many investments in what may be called "securities," or monetary instruments. But you need not worry about the jargon; all you need to know is that any category of item you might have considered investing in directly is likely available for you to invest in by using a mutual fund. One of the points of a fund is that you have someone looking after your interests full-time. For instance, managers might sell stocks if they decide the company is not doing well and the value of them will drop, all with no intervention on your part.

It is in the interest of the fund managers to try to obtain the best return for their investors, as this contributes to their own success and reputation. If more people are attracted to their fund because of its performance, then they can demand and receive a better salary without increasing the operating cost of the fund, as their remuneration is usually expressed as a percent of the total fund. You might also find that some managers use their performance in one company to get a better position in another and, particularly with the younger fund companies, the manager's résumé is often used as qualification.

A further advantage of investing through a mutual fund is that the manager may be able to invest in ways that are not available to the individual, especially because he or she is able to make relatively massive investments. As professionals, managers are also likely to hear about opportunities that you may not, as well as a staff of researchers whose full-time job is to stay on top of the securities markets, allowing them to invest your money more efficiently than if you tried to do it yourself.

You may be concerned about giving so much responsibility to one person. But be assured that there are significant regulations surrounding the formation and running of a mutual fund, and these protect you from any illegal actions. This is in contrast to some other fund varieties, such as hedge funds, where there is much less oversight.

Shares

Many mutual funds have a large holding of stocks in their collective portfolio. Stocks and shares are traded every business day around the world and represent a massive marketplace. A share is literally a share of ownership in a publicly traded company, and shareholders have some say in how the company is run, usually at an Annual General Meeting.

When the owners of a company decide to "go public" — that is, to sell shares to the general public to raise money for their operation — an initial public offering (IPO) is undertaken. On the day of the offering, anyone can buy shares at the initial price until they are all sold. If all goes well, the company will raise the money it needs to satisfy plans.

After this day, the company has little to do directly with the buying and selling of the shares. The shares are traded on a stock market between investors, which have no impact on the company's operation. The value of the shares can vary, depending on how much the investors think they are worth. The company can choose to give a dividend — that is, a share of their profits — regularly to their shareholders, and many of the larger companies do.

The shares have a value depending on the marketplace. If a dividend is paid, then this can be compared to how much invested money can earn in savings account interest to see whether it represents a reasonable return on the money. It is more difficult to put a value on a share when the company does not pay a dividend. In this case, it is more the expectation of dividends that may be paid in the future that drives the price and, ultimately, what other investors will pay to buy the shares that controls the value.

The only other interaction the company may have with the stock market is if it needs to raise more capital, which can be done by issuing more shares or choosing to buy some of the shares back.

The stock market has been through some rocky times in recent years, including the technology crash at the beginning of this century, as well as the major credit crisis at the end of 2008, which has been compared to the Great Depression. When stocks lose value, it is described as a "bear market," in which buy-and-hold investors lose money — think of a bear swinging with his paws and knocking down the prices. The opposite of this is called a "bull market," in which values are rising and most investors make money. To remember this term, think of a bull throwing prices up with his horns.

Occasionally, even a large company can encounter a serious financial problem, such as the case of General Motors® at the end of 2008. Over many years, General Motors has incurred increasingly higher debts and liabilities and has shown an inability to make any inroads into paying off its debts. At the time of this writing, the liabilities amount to about $172.8 billion, including retirement accounts and other commitments, and the capitalization of the company is under $1 billion, which is inadequate for continued operation. This led to its filing of bankruptcy in June 2009.

Ultimately, if a company goes bankrupt, stockholders are unlikely to receive any of their money back. The bankruptcy proceedings include paying back pennies on the dollar to its creditors, as well as paying the bond holders who lent the company money. Stockholders are at the bottom of the list for collecting on any funds remaining.

Having said that, buying stocks is historically recognized as the way that has increased invested money at the greatest rate, when compared to other investments. The drawback when investing in stocks is that they should be held for some years; they should not be a place to put your money if you may need it next year. The fluctuations in the price of stocks can continue for several years, and if you need to withdraw your funds, it may be the wrong time. It can take five or ten years to recover from a slump.

Of course, when you invest in stocks via a mutual fund, you expect and depend on the manager of the fund to sell the stocks before they lose too much value in a bear market. You also expect the manager to diversify the fund's holding so that an issue with any particular company will have a negligible effect on the overall value of the mutual fund. As seen in recent history, sometimes fund managers do not perform much better than the average investor, which is why stock-based funds are regarded as riskier than some other investments — regardless of who is in control.

Large Cap

A large-cap, or large-capitalization, company includes a substantial company such as General Electric or IBM®. Because of the size of these companies, shares in large-cap companies are regarded as fairly safe, and mutual funds based on large-cap investments are low risk. The term "large cap" is relative to other companies in the market.

The capitalization of a company can be easily figured out by knowing how many shares have been issued and what the market value of each share is on any particular day. Sometimes, large companies are defined as those valued at more than $10 billion. Morningstar®, at **www.morningstar.com**, is a well-respected stock-market analysis company that provides detailed information and evaluations of many financial instruments. Their preferred definition for a large-cap company is one in which the market capitalization falls in the largest 70 percent for their region, with region referring to a geographical area, such as the United States or Europe.

Medium Cap

A medium-cap company, as you might expect, has a smaller valuation. Some say these companies' valuations are in the range from $2 billion to $10 billion; Morningstar says that these companies fall in the next 20 percent of market cap. These are still substantial companies and are considered fairly safe places to invest your money.

Small Cap

Small-cap companies are anything valued at less than $2 billion, or the smallest 10 percent of the market capitalization. These include everything from the start-up public companies at a minimal valuation on up, and even though Morningstar only includes 10 percent of market cap in this bracket, there are many more small-cap companies than there are large-cap organizations because each company's capitalization is much smaller. Because of their nature, these are considered much riskier investments.

In addition to the level of risk, small companies behave differently from large companies and may even increase in value when large companies are declining, or vice versa. Also, if they pay any dividend, small companies tend to pay much less, but can appreciate in value more than the bigger companies.

Growth

Apart from classification by size — in other words, market capitalization — companies can be classified with regard to their characteristics. The shares of a company that is rapidly expanding and generating larger profits are referred to as "growth stocks." This means that these companies tend to pay less out in dividends, as they use the money to pay for the expansion. The stocks are likely to be fairly expensive but, in view of the expansion, they will grow in value.

Value

In contrast to growth stocks, value stocks tend to be cheap compared to the company's assets and profits. The idea in this case is simply to buy the stock and wait until the marketplace realizes the true worth, increasing your investment. Simply put, an investor in value stocks is looking for a bargain. It is possible for stocks to be both growth and value, but it is not common.

International

The mutual fund may concentrate on stocks from the United States or may be diversified — partly or wholly — into the international market. These may be called "overseas funds." When the home market is going through a lackluster period, there may be opportunities to be found abroad. In addition, foreign stocks introduce the question of currency exchange rates, and if the dollar is not well regarded and falling in value against other currencies, additional profit is available for the overseas investor.

Although the international funds are viewed differently, they still comprise the same elements as the domestic funds, such as small or large cap. Overseas investing may involve different laws for the fund manager, but because you will be buying a fund in this country, this makes no difference to you.

A concern you might have is that investing in foreign companies is in some way being disloyal or unpatriotic. In this respect, the truth is that we live in a global economy, and it is difficult for most people to buy American-only on a regular basis. The dwindling amount of goods we produce at home is a concern for our economy as a whole, which is rapidly becoming heavily service-dependent and, therefore, less wealth-creating. Regardless of whether you invest in mutual funds with overseas holdings, there will be minimal impact to our economy when compared to other larger factors.

Bonds

A bond has a maturity date, making it similar to the certificate of deposit (CD) that you may be familiar with purchasing from a bank.

When you purchase a bond, you will know the interest rate that will be paid and the date on which the bond will be paid back with the interest. For example, a company may issue a bond for five years that will pay 6 percent a year. As long as the company is viable and does not have a financial catastrophe, you are fairly certain to get your money back with interest.

Fascinatingly, the prevailing interest rate can affect the purchase price of a bond. When the generally available current interest rate goes down, the price of a bond will go up above its face value, and vice versa. To understand why this happens, consider the following example:

Suppose you have a bond that matures in five years and pays 6 percent interest per a year, and say the face value of this bond is $100. This means that each year, you will receive $6 in interest, paid to your account, because the bond has a face value of $100. If you hold the bond to the end, also known as the maturity date, you will get the $100 of capital paid back to you.

If the interest that is generally available in other investments to a current investor falls to 4 percent, think now about what would happen to this bond. If the bond could be bought for the face value of $100, everybody would want one to get the higher interest — the 6 percent promised — and supply would not be able to keep up with demand. Therefore, investors would be prepared to pay more than the face value of $100, and the current bond owners would demand a higher price.

Perhaps the bond could be bought for $110, which is $10 more than the face value. In this case, the buyer would receive $6 each year for five years and get $100 repaid at the end of the five years for a total of $130, which is $20 greater than the initial investment. The available alternative is a 4-percent bond that sells at face value of $100. The buyer would spend $100, receive $4 each year for five years, and then get his or her $100 back. Again, this would mean making $20 over the initial investment.

This is a simple example and, in practice, the generally accepted present value of a bond at a different rate of interest can be calculated by financial experts. It partly depends on what you want to receive from your investment. In the 6 percent case above, a 10 percent increase in investment would bring you 50 percent more interest each year, greatly boosting your cash flow, even though the total return was similar.

There are two factors by which the performance of a bond is measured. One of them is the interest rate sensitivity, as explained above, also sometimes called the duration of the bond. The sensitivity to the interest rate, or by how much the price of the bond varies when the interest rate changes, is related to how long it is before maturity. The second factor is the obvious question of the credit quality of the company — for example, how likely you are to get the money paid back at the maturity date.

Prior to recent times, it has been typical to look at the ratings of various companies with the expectation that they provide an indication of the soundness of the company. Unfortunately, the subprime crisis in the credit markets has exposed the inadequacy of some rating methodologies and has caused some surprises in terms of which companies are sound and which may be verging on bankruptcy. Nonetheless, while they should be viewed with a grain of salt, the ratings of the credit rating firms, such as Standard & Poor's and Moody's, are perhaps the best indication.

For instance, the Standard & Poor's rating system has a highest grade of "AAA," meaning you can be fairly confident that the company rated in this manner will make all the interest payments and return the principal at maturity on any bonds they issue. Bonds with any "A" rating, or even a "BBB" rating, are called "investment grade" and are also regarded as sound places to put your money.

Lower-rated bonds are sometimes called high-yield bonds or "junk bonds," which, though not a flattering title, does convey the idea that repayment may not be forthcoming. The bonds must be issued at a higher yield to attract investment, given the greater risk that they will default. If there is a recession, these bonds will lose more value due to the exposure to risk in a down-turning economy.

An alternative are Government-issued bonds, which tend to be regarded as creditworthy — particularly as the government is in control of the money supply and must be considered able to repay any of its debts.

Short-Term

One of the basic facts about a bond is how many years there are until it matures. As mentioned above, the duration of the bond is related to the number of years, with short-term bonds less sensitive to sudden changes in interest rate. In this context, "short-term" is considered to be just a few years out. If the interest rate generally available changes, the short-term bond will not vary significantly in its value.

When purchasing a mutual fund that specializes in bond funds, you will usually be able to ask whether the manager is concentrating on short-term funds or otherwise. Carefully evaluate the answer you receive, as there is no easy definition of the difference between short, medium, and long-term bonds.

Medium-Term

Medium-term bonds are widely considered to be less than ten years, but more than five. You should expect that the interest rate offered on the medium-term bonds is higher than you would get on the short-term, as they are considered riskier because their value is more affected by interest rate variations. These bonds are sometimes called "intermediate-term bonds."

Long-Term

Because of the reasons given before, long-term bonds tend to give a higher yield than the others for a given level of risk. In approximate terms, long-term bonds are regarded as greater than ten years and may take as much as 20 years to maturity. These bonds will vary the most when the interest rate generally available fluctuates, and the duration of the bond will give a direct indication of the sensitivity.

For instance, a long-term bond with a duration of 14 years will be about twice as sensitive to interest rate changes as a medium-term bond with a duration of seven years. Note that duration is not the same as time to maturity. It can be calculated mathematically and should be available from the bond administrator. Often people refer to the time to maturity, but this is not as accurate an indication of the sensitivity to interest rate fluctuations.

Treasury

U.S. Treasury bonds are regarded as inherently safer than any other. Because of this, do not expect the highest levels of return when choosing to invest in these. The advantage of using a mutual fund to invest in Treasury bonds is that you have liquidity, whereas if you invest directly in them, you may have trouble realizing your capital quickly.

Keep in mind that in 1997, the government issued a new type of bond that is inflation indexed, which are investable either directly or through a mutual fund. The interest rate appears very low, but whether these bonds are worthwhile depends on how much inflation there is.

Depending on your view of future inflation, you may decide that these are a worthwhile investment. But an unfortunate part of these inflation-indexed bonds is that the government has, in recent years, tinkered with the way it measures inflation, and this means that the inflation index may not fully reflect the inflation that you experience. Also note that inflation-indexed Treasury bonds only pay out the stated rate of interest each year, and the amount deemed for inflation is added to the redemption amount at the end of the term, meaning they are not the best choice for investors looking for a steady income.

Municipal

Another interesting choice is the municipal bond, sometimes called the "muni." This is issued by state or local governments and will come with special tax advantages if you live in the issuing state. Income from the bond tends to be free of state taxes, and even if you do not live in the issuing state, income from a municipal bond is often free of federal taxes.

However, this is not necessarily an advantage to you, depending on whether you are retired and investing in the fund through a tax vehicle, such as a retirement account. Look at the overall picture to see how to secure the best returns for your situation.

Other Investments

Although stocks and bonds are the mainstay of mutual fund investment managers, there are a few other types of financial investments, which you can find used in specialist mutual funds.

Real Estate

For your personal investment portfolio, you may have considered putting some money into other things. For instance, many people will look at buying real estate, perhaps to become a landlord and derive rental income. In better times than we are experiencing presently, the real estate investor would also expect a regular increase in the value of this property, and such capital appreciation has been a tempting incentive.

Direct investing in real estate is outside the scope of this book, but I believe that some measure of your wealth should be diversified into this area. The actual returns that can be achieved vary greatly depending on what part of the country you are in, but because you can borrow readily to buy housing, you can leverage your initial deposit and see appreciable returns. Of course, this is not guaranteed, and the events of 2007, 2008, and 2009 have created an atmosphere of caveat emptor when it comes to buying real estate.

The number of foreclosures and the reduction in price of real estate has made it an attractive investment for those who feel that a recovery will soon take hold, but this is a view that investors must assess for themselves. It is certain that many people will not rely on regular capital appreciation for some time to come.

If you wish to invest in real estate without having to organize renters, pay property taxes, make repairs, and fulfill other similar obligations, then you can do so through a special type of fund called a Real Estate Investment Trust (REIT), which comprises stocks of companies that invest in real estate. These companies often invest in commercial real estate rather than individual residential properties.

Commonly, the real estate at hand may be shopping centers, malls, or apartment buildings. If you are prepared to do the research, as an individual you can invest directly in a REIT, which has historically been a fairly successful niche. If you would rather have a mutual fund manager do the homework and discover what he or she thinks are the most profitable opportunities, then you can purchase a mutual fund that specializes in investing in REITs.

Collectibles

Another area many are saying is a safe haven for money is in the purchasing of collectible items, particularly art. While many items are created and sold as collectible as a marketing exercise, buying quality goods and antiques is another avenue for investment in goods that are material and can retain their value.

Again, outside the scope of this book, if you are interested in making some investments in collectibles, you would be well advised to seek professional advice, as there are many variables that can radically affect the value of particular items. As the value of the items you are considering buying increases, you must enlist more caution with regard to determining that you have a first-rate example of the item — one that will, in all likelihood, increase in value.

Because of the individual nature of collectible items, this is not a market sector in which you will find a mutual fund.

Commodities

You may think of commodities as a generic term for items in which traders deal, such as coffee beans or crude oil. In a broader sense, commodities are anything with a uniform supply across the market — in other words, when you buy rice or copper, you know what to expect. This would not be the case if you bought, for instance, a car from one person or another, as it is likely there would be differences between them.

Certainly commodities are traded in large quantities by people who need the raw materials, such as cereal manufacturers or pipe makers. There is also what is called the "futures market," in which people commit to supplying or to buying commodities at a set date in the future. While many who have heard of it associate a great deal of risk with trading "futures," there is also the opportunity for large profits.

The original purpose of futures was to provide a hedge so that, for instance, beef producers can be sure of the price they pay for cattle feed, and can also lock in the price at which they can sell the meat. This allows planning ahead, which stabilizes the economy.

While you may not have considered trading futures, you may have considered dealing in commodities. For instance, it is well-known that investors seek out gold when they are concerned about the performance of the stock market or when it is perceived that the dollar will be weak on the international currency exchange. While in the past government intervention has affected the value of gold, many prefer to be able to have and hold the physical metal, regarding it as safer than a paper promise.

But what many people do not take into account is that there is no interest paid on holding the physical metal, and the value over a long period keeps pace with inflation, unlike wiser investments, which will give higher returns.

However, you can invest in gold and silver with a special type of mutual fund, which is more convenient than taking possession of gold bullion — which is heavy, subject to theft, and cannot be easily traced. These funds are subject to large fluctuations, thus they are better for the active trader who is in touch with the market. For investors who want a stable fund, a mutual bond fund is more likely to satisfy their needs.

Other Fund Factors

With thousands of mutual funds available, you can find funds to suit virtually any investment desire you have. As long as the securities that the fund invests in are regularly traded, commercially viable securities, someone has likely set up a fund for it.

One of the niche areas for investment is "socially responsible investment." There is no definition of this and, in many ways, what is socially responsible is in the eye of the beholder. If you are interested in such investments, make your own investigations into the philosophies of the fund managers and determine for yourself if you believe the fund is acting in a more socially responsible way than others.

For some companies, it may be easy to say they are not socially responsible. For instance, investing in tobacco companies — despite the funding that they now give to support anti-smoking campaigns — is, in some people's opinion, not a responsible action. One could take a similar view toward brewers and wine and spirit manufacturers when considering the number of deaths caused by drunken driving, but it is arguable that it is only the irresponsible use of their products that is harmful, unlike smoking, which harms when used as intended.

Sean Hyman has significant experience in many financial fields and is in demand for his expertise. Here is his advice:

CASE STUDY: SEAN HYMAN

Sean Hyman has an extensive background in the financial markets that extends more than 15 years. Over his career, Hyman has been a stock broker, manager of a team of stock brokers, a course instructor in the currency markets, a financial writer, and key speaker at conferences, both nationally and internationally. You can follow Hyman's articles at **www.Moneynews.com**, **www.sovereignsociety.com**, **www.DailyFX.com**, **www.myWealth.com**, and **www. SeekingAlpha.com**. You can also follow him on **www. YouTube.com**.

To contact Hyman for articles or speaking engagements, e-mail him at shm-cc2000@hotmail.com

How did you get into mutual fund investing?

When I was very young, I had heard horror stories about investing in individual stocks. Back then, I knew very little, so it was a safer starting point to be in mutual funds since they are more diverse.

Later on, when I learned about technical analysis, I found that it was easier to technically trade mutual funds. Since they are only priced once a day and don't trade intraday, I could do that and have a day job, too.

So I would search out very volatile mutual funds, especially mutual funds that held positions in the market leaders. Then, I would use my technical signals to time my buys. By learning how to become better about my points of entry into a fund, it helped me to not waste time getting back to break-even. Instead, I was able to maximize that time and grow my portfolio much quicker.

As an investor, what do you see as your primary function when selecting investments?

I look for mutual funds that hold high growth stocks in sectors that are leading the way at the time. I also consider where we are at in the business/economic cycle. There are certain sectors of the economy that do better at certain phases of the economic cycle than at other times.

This is a more advanced technique and not the easiest place to start out. However, searching out top fund managers with a good track record that have a knack for choosing high-growth stocks is a great place to start.

CASE STUDY: SEAN HYMAN

My thoughts are...if that fund manager is good at picking the stocks, and you're good at timing his fund, then you can actually exceed his return. This is how I would exceed the return of the fund manager. I let him do all of the "hard work" of picking the stocks to be in the fund, and I just timed when to make my purchases.

Rather than just dollar-cost averaging at a certain time each month (like most mutual fund investors do), I would use technical indicators, like Bollinger Bands or the Slow Stochastics, to decide when to make purchases into the fund. For those that are willing to learn technical analysis, it can give you an added edge in your investing over the long haul.

Given the current state of the financial markets, have you changed the way that you select any investments, or is your existing strategy already coping well?

Yes! There were times when I would buy some funds just because they were beaten down. Not any more! They have to be breaking into a new uptrend now or they are not even considered. In the end, I will make out fine on those, since they are long-term investments ... but time was wasted by not picking funds that were already in an uptrend or beginning an uptrend at that moment.

Even in the recent bear market, there were mutual funds that were going up. They were few in number. For instance, there were funds that invested in gold, and gold stocks that were headed upward even in the recent global recession. So they are out there. You just have to search them out.

What do you like and dislike about mutual funds?

I do not like it that a fund manager can pass down taxable gains to you even though you weren't along for the ride during the times that those taxable gains were made. I also do not like loaded funds or funds that require large initial investments. What I do like about mutual funds is that they are one of the most practical investments for those on Main Street to invest in. You do not have to know all the ins and outs of balance sheets, and it's not a requirement to be a good stock picker.

These are all the things that the fund manager does for you. So you can just put up the money and let them do the hard work.

So while I took a more active role in my own mutual fund investing, it is not a requirement to do so much of that

CASE STUDY: SEAN HYMAN

What is the biggest success you have had concerning mutual funds?.

Here is a story about one of the fastest gains I have had. I had a friend that was about to get married. She only had a few thousand dollars and was only going to be able to have an OK wedding. Being young and brave, I talked her into allowing me to trade the money for her. In only a few months, I had it up to $10,000 by compounding the winnings. Keep in mind… this was a very volatile mutual fund. It was the first of the funds that contained derivative contracts in it to enhance the returns. Needless to say, she had a very good wedding!

In my mind, mutual fund trading is still safer than individual stock trading because it removed some of the risk that can come with being in one stock at a time. This fund I used was diverse, but nonetheless on the edge for mutual fund investing. So I looked at this as being more risky than the average mutual fund, but also less risky than the average stock. So it was a good middle ground for my comfort zone at the time.

What is the biggest challenge that you have had to face?

It would have to be investing in bear markets. This is the toughest time to be in the markets for sure. There are more surprises from companies that cause you to have to dodge more bullets then when there is a bull market.

Also, I have learned to not use margin or buy leveraged mutual funds (ones that contain derivative contracts) in bear markets.

What advice would you give to potential investors, particularly in the face of the economic crisis, and how would this vary depending on their age?

Investors get in and out of investments at the worst times. They only buy when they have heard the financial news media talk about how much the stock market has gone up. By that time, that bull market is usually at least half over. Second, they exit based off of fear versus being logical.

One thing is for certain. More recessions will come. More bear markets will come as a result. However, money is still made through the years because bull markets generally last much longer than bear markets. Corporate America still grows over time despite recessions. However, people get caught up in the moment, and they lose their heads and sell out of their funds and guarantee themselves a loss.

CASE STUDY: SEAN HYMAN

If you believe that corporations in America will continue to grow over time, and that ten and 20 years from now, America will be further down the road than it is now, then you should hold onto your funds even through recessions, if you are a long-term investor.

If you have ten years until retirement, you have to start adjusting your portfolio much more conservatively. If you have only five years until retirement, you really need to have much bigger stakes in bonds and bond funds than in stock mutual funds. Also, of stock funds, as you near retirement, it would benefit you to own funds that hold high-dividend-paying stocks rather than riskier, high-growth stocks.

If you are young and have 20+ years until retirement, then these are your years to be aggressive in your investing. As you get older and closer to retirement, you will lose this right to invest aggressively. Some young people make the mistake of investing too conservatively at the beginning of their careers, just like some investors that are nearing retirement are still investing way too aggressively and don't realize it until they get hit hard in the next bear market.

CHAPTER 5

Checking Up on Fund Performance

Though you have now selected the right funds for your circumstances; determined the mix that you want between safe low-return funds and riskier, higher-yielding mutual funds; and selected the best of each type of mutual fund with the help of the earlier chapters, there is still work to do.

While one of the advantages of a mutual fund is that you are not required to maintain constant contact with the gains and losses of individual securities — that is the fund manager's role — this does not mean you should not regularly review how your funds are doing. However, past performance should not be taken as an indication of future results. Though history may be all that we have to go on when accessing the fund's suitability for an investment portfolio, factors can change, and your needs can change, too. Consequently, you should plan to examine the performance of the individual funds that you hold at regular intervals, review the performance of other similar funds, and determine whether you need to make any changes.

You should undertake a thorough review of your holdings each year and make a cursory review every quarter. That is not to say that you will decide to change your investment strategy if a particular quarter — or even a year of performance — is not the best in its class. No one can tell which fund will prove to be the absolute best in any future time period. However, the funds that you hold should perform well compared to the best; otherwise, it is time to sort them out.

One of the functions you may want to consider when you do checkups is whether you need to rebalance your allocations. Standard practice is to reduce the proportion of stocks in your portfolio as you age and retirement approaches because stocks are more volatile and, if you are relying on taking your money out in a year or two, you could be caught out with a down cycle in the stock market. Biasing your investment toward bonds when you may become more reliant on being able to access the funds is a sensible choice.

In addition to your choice to rebalance the proportion of stocks and bonds, as well as other monetary instruments in your portfolio, you may find that you need to rebalance because of performance. After all, the higher risk funds should give greater returns most of the time — that is the expectation and trade-off. Consequently, in a typical schedule with reinvestment in the funds, you may find that your holdings in the riskier investments will increase. Every year, review the percentages you have in different types of holdings and bring them back to the starting proportions.

The Review

Every three months, schedule time to briefly review your mutual fund holdings. While the first aspect you might look at is which funds have performed the best and which the worst, in this relatively short time period there will be fluctuations and, unless there is something drastic afoot, you should not change your fund on the basis of these numbers.

It is important to compare your fund's performance with the performance of similar ones. After all, you cannot expect a money market fund to behave like a stock mutual fund, and you should know how your particular selection is performing in comparison with its peers. The money market fund is in your portfolio for a purpose related to risk and diversification and, if it has not performed well, it still deserves its place if it was one of the better money market funds available.

If you do notice a drastic problem with your portfolio, further examine if there is an underlying reason to change allocation in midyear. For example, if you find that the manager of the fund responsible for the performance in the last decade — on which you based your original selection — has decided to leave that position, and the newly appointed manager does not seem to have the same finesse and knowledge, it may be appropriate to switch out this fund to the one you previously selected as second-best.

Other items that could cause a major change might be your mutual fund company merging with another or any issued statements that suggest that the direction of the fund is being changed. Barring any major upheavals such as these, you should most often leave the unit allocation alone until the annual review.

The annual review should be a bigger proposition, in which you will thoroughly examine the performance of your funds and that of similar funds, should you be evaluating them for a potential change. Your first step should be to prepare a table or spreadsheet that allows you to break out the categories of your investment and total them. You can use the recognized categories, such as large value and small-cap growth and, using spreadsheet functions or a manual method, total these to reveal your current investment allocation.

The most important proportions you first review will be the amount of money you have in shares, the percentage in bonds, and the remaining sum that is in money market or cash equivalent funds. You can use various guidelines to determine what percentage of stocks you should hold at any particular age, and a typical one is that the percentage of bonds you hold is the same as your age. For instance, at age 30, you would have 30 percent of your investment in bonds and the rest in stocks, whereas at age 70, a full 70 percent of your money might be in bonds, with only 30 percent in stocks. However, this guideline is widely viewed as conservative.

While it may seem simple and reassuring to have experts decide your stock and bond allocation for you, such guidelines seldom take account of your lifestyle, job security, and personal risk tolerance. Starting with the guidelines, try to decide what allocation you are comfortable with. This can change from year to year, as circumstances change and as you grow older, and this will be part of your annual fund review.

Your annual review should be thorough and include assessing the various market sectors that you are invested in and to what extent. Again, diversification is recommended, so you will find that some of your investments do not perform as well as others, but spreading the risk is the prime purpose of diversification to avoid any unforeseen disasters.

While looking at the makeup of your funds, also consider how much you have invested in overseas stocks. You must be careful when you look at your funds, as sometimes the names are not truly indicative of where the investing emphasis lies. For example, you may find that a domestic investing fund actually has some internationally based holdings. Break down your foreign funds to see what countries are represented so that you are not surprised should there be a sudden currency devaluation in a particular country.

You may also come across a contrary view that states that you should be in the fashionable market sector and chase the highest gaining type of investment. Proponents argue that this will improve your portfolio's performance. Whether you consider this a viable alternative likely depends, again, on your risk profile. I cannot recommend it for the typical investor looking to have a secure nest egg, but if you are prepared to work hard and take a chance on your retirement, then better returns can be available with this method.

Delving deeper into the mutual fund holding can be a sensible exercise. Depending on what type of funds you hold, they may be investing in the same companies, and you may find that you are not as diversified as you initially thought. Particularly if your portfolio includes several large-cap funds, you might find that several are holding General Electric or Microsoft® shares, and that weakness in just one company could affect you across the board. Investigate the fund's holdings and total up the major stocks that may be excessive.

If you find that you have more than 5 percent of your portfolio in any one company, you may be too exposed and should consider making some adjustments. If you also invest individually in the shares, it would be easy to sell the excess, but if you hold more than 5 percent in the combined holdings of your mutual funds, then you may need to do more calculation to determine which funds to adjust.

It may be difficult to rebalance a portfolio heavily. After all, this process entails selling some of the funds that have been perform-ing well, as these are the ones that have grown larger than their required allocation, and instead putting your money into funds that have not performed so well. This can be a challenging exer-cise unless you approach it in a mechanical, relentless fashion. Remember that you are protecting the high gains you have had in the best-performing funds by taking the money away before the securities contained in them slip back in price.

An alternative approach that can be more palatable is keeping the money you currently have in the high-performing funds. To rebalance your portfolio, you direct new investment to the funds that are under-represented, thus you increase their percentage holding and invest more, which should always be your aim.

Also note that correcting the odd percentage variation from your ideal allocation is not a stringent requirement. You can set a limit that the allocation can vary before you go through the trouble of changing your holdings. For instance, you may say that anything up to 5 percent variation from your ideal allocation is not worth changing.

CHAPTER 6

Costs and Fees

Although many investors are aware of the costs of their cable television or their telephone bills, statistics show that many are not aware of all the costs involved in their investments. This is not surprising, as some of the costs are hidden and, if you do not actively research your fund, some of them will escape your attention.

Someone must pay for the establishment that runs a mutual fund, and this money has to come from the investors, as the only source of income. The actual amount it costs to run the fund varies depending on the efficiency of the investment company. Because the costs are shared among all shareholders, the more popular the fund is and the greater the number of investors, the less each individual investor pays out of his or her account each year.

None of the fees should be kept a secret from you, but some are more openly revealed than others. You will find that there may be fees that you do not incur because of the nature of your holding; for instance, there are fees in some funds that switch between similar funds in the same investment company. The following is a summary of the fees that you will want to examine as part of your assessment of which funds to invest in.

The underlying investments, whether they be shares, bonds, or other securities, are crucial to the return that you may expect. But the variation in fees, and particularly the unexpected fees or fees that are not charged by all funds, can eat into your profits over the longer term.

Operating Expenses

Operating expenses are incurred by all mutual funds, and the numbers on these tend to be easily available, as the SEC requires the details to be published. Found in the fund's prospectus, these are the costs that are incurred so that the fund can do business, and they cannot be avoided. There is a range in operating expenses, varying from a fraction of a percent of the fund's capitalization, up to 2 or 3 percent. This reflects the amount of work required to manage the fund; for instance, index funds will normally be expected to have lower costs than funds that actively trade stocks.

It is usual for the operating expenses to be expressed as a percentage of the average assets of the fund for any particular year, and this number is called the "expense ratio." This standard basis allows comparison between different mutual funds, and although there can be many other fees and costs, the operating expense is universal; consequently, it is often incorrectly used as the only basis of deciding whether a fund is costly.

When looking for a money market fund or a similar, relatively safe fund with a modest return, check for an operating expense in the region of 0.5 percent or less. These funds are not difficult to run, and if they are only making, say, 5 percent return in a year, they cannot afford to charge high expenses; otherwise, they will not attract investors from comparable funds. These funds tend to choose to invest in quality bonds with short maturity dates, thus they are not prone to large fluctuations with interest rate adjustments.

Moving up in the expected returns, the next class of funds would invest in regular bonds and, if these are not in a specialized field, such as emerging markets, you should be able to find funds that charge no more than 0.75 percent annual expenses. On the other hand, if the fund is investing in higher yielding bonds that require specialized knowledge, you may pay up to 1 percent in expenses each year.

The next class of funds you may invest in include stocks and, because of the returns and the expertise needed to manage these funds, many of them charge for 1 or 2 percent in operating expenses. Again, for specialized knowledge in particular areas of study investment, you may find that you must pay even more. If you search around, you should be able to find similar funds that may charge only 1.5 percent per year.

Management Fees

The term "management fees" usually includes several of the following itemized fees. It is a broad term covering all the costs required to run the office and administration of the fund, apart from those that are separately billed. The fees include factors that are not easily itemized, such as administration staff wages, toner for the copying machine, utility bills, and all other costs normally incurred when running a business. The following items are ones that can be separately distinguished.

Investment Advisory Fees

The money in the fund will pay an investment advisor or management team for their services, and this amount includes research staff and other resources. The investment advisor will also be responsible for producing financial statements and determining the value of the fund's shares.

As such, this is a core cost for the mutual fund, and this is where you may notice the difference between the percentages charged by different types of funds, such as the lower-cost for an index fund, which requires less decision-making and management. This fee may be in the region of half a percent of the fund's value each year.

Audit Fees

As required by law in order to regulate and control the mutual fund, the fund will be audited each year. This must be done by an independent firm of accountants that is not a subsidiary of the investment company to ensure that the process is honest.

Directors' Fees

The directors of the fund are entitled to receive recompense for their time and traveling expenses. These are necessarily incurred, as the directors must meet at regular intervals to discuss the operation of the fund and ensure it is meeting objectives. If they are employees of the fund, they usually do not receive additional compensation for acting as directors.

The directors are the overseers of the fund and can appoint or dismiss the fund manager, depending on his or her performance. It is their job to set compensation and ensure the fund is following the direction expected by the investors.

SEC Fees

As a regulating body, the SEC charges fees to the fund for allowing it to operate. There will sometimes be further fees to regulating agencies, such as state agencies, as part of the required dues for licensing and continued operation of a mutual fund.

Report Expenses

A mutual fund should issue a report detailing its current situation and holdings at least every year. Many funds issue reports more frequently, although often in less detail, and the cost of preparation, printing, and mailing will be part of the overall operating expenses.

12b-1 Fees

Authorized in 1980, this fee is optional and is seldom charged by a no-load fund. The fee was created so that the fund can charge for the costs of marketing and distribution as a separate item to the management fee. As such, if charged, it is a continuing operating expense.

It is worth noting that if the fund does not currently have a 12b-1 plan and has not included it in literature to date, then it requires a vote of the investors as shareholders in the fund for it to be instigated. Whether it is charged should be found in the mutual fund prospectus.

Redemption Fees

Redemption fees are charged by some mutual funds but can be avoided by selecting different funds that are otherwise similar. The redemption fee is charged when you decide to sell your holding in the fund and redeem your investment.

Some believe redemption fees were invented to provide a disincentive for investors to change funds frequently. Whatever the reason for their creation, there seems to be little reason to support a fund that charges such fees.

These fees are, to one way of thinking, the opposite of the load levied by load funds. The fee is charged when you sell your shares in a fund, otherwise known as "redeeming" them. The redemption fee is often set at one half of one percent of the value redeemed, and this will eat into any profits that you may have made in the fund.

The prospectus should detail any redemption fees charged by the fund, and you will find this in the section of the prospectus that advises you how to redeem your shares for cash.

Switching Fees

Switching fees can be incurred when you decide to change your mutual fund holding from one fund to another fund run by the same investment company. In other words, you are switching your holding from one mutual fund to another. As with redemption fees, the charges exist primarily to discourage frequent changing.

The idea of switching fees is a fairly recent one as, for many years, funds permitted ready exchange of allocation within the fund family. However, this does involve the funds in administrative costs to keep track of your holdings and to implement the changes, as well as to send out notices of confirmation. In this respect, it is reasonable of the fund to charge you extra if you choose to use this facility; otherwise, such costs would be spread over all investors, which could be considered unfair.

It is not clear whether switching fees will become more popular, as investors may tend to choose funds that do not require the fees. This may make the funds that charge them reconsider whether they are losing business by imposing the switching fees.

Maintenance Fees

If a mutual fund lists a separate maintenance fee to be charged to your account, the best advice is to carefully consider whether you want to invest in this fund or find an equivalent with similar performance. A routine maintenance fee that does not serve a special function or request may be an addition that should already be included in the operating expenses.

As part of the expenses that the mutual fund imposes as "necessary," any maintenance fee will be detailed in the prospectus. Often, it is stated to be a flat annual charge, which will be automatically deducted from any dividend payouts. It is up to you to spot this required expense before investing.

Loads

As previously mentioned, one basic decision to make when selecting a mutual fund is whether to buy a load fund or a no-load fund. In this respect, the mutual fund company is forthright in advising you as to whether these charges will be made, and you can make your decision accordingly. This is in contrast to some of the fees mentioned above, which you may have found out about later if you had not been alerted to them.

A load is another name for a sales commission, which is an amount added to the share price in order to pay the salespeople or brokers who sell you shares in the mutual fund. In other words, when you buy the shares, you pay the net asset value plus the load for each share. You may be surprised at how high a load can be — as much as 8.5 percent of the purchase price. Even if there are no fees for the sale of the shares, you will need a significant increase in value in order to break even.

Even if you attempt to buy the mutual fund shares directly from the company and avoid this charge, the company will charge you the same amount and keep the commission. While there is no doubt that someone performing work for the investment company in selling their shares should be recompensed, it is best to avoid such a direct reduction in your initial investment.

The argument has long been made that when you pay more, you experience better performance, thus the rumor has spread that load funds are a superior product with better management, which may compensate for the additional cost.

The Institute for Econometric Research, founded in 1971 and sold to *Time* magazine in 1998, undertook a 25-year study that showed conclusively that no load funds actually give better returns, even before allowing for the sales charges or loads. The study took place between 1971 and 1996 and examined the growth in no-load mutual funds, compared with all mutual funds in that period.

In the given time, taken as a whole over the 25 years, the no-load mutual funds gave an average annual return of just over 12 percent. In contrast, when all the mutual funds were considered together, they only returned an average of 10.6 percent per year. Though this study is dated now, no convincing argument has yet been made to assert that load funds perform any differently today and consequently, with the multiple choices that are available in the marketplace, there seems no significant reason to invest in load funds.

CHAPTER 7

The Advantages of Mutual Fund Investment

J ust glancing at all the fees that you can incur when using mutual funds for your investment vehicle, you might wonder whether you would be better off investing in the individual securities. But to do so would mean denying yourself access to two of the greatest features of using a mutual fund for your savings.

Research

The mutual fund manager is a professional who commits his or her life's work to selecting stocks, bonds, or other securities to the best of his ability. Often he or she is a Chartered Financial Analyst and has many years' experience in analyzing investments. In addition, the manager often works with a team of researchers who are able to contribute more work than you are able to in order to stay on top of their fund holdings.

Consider for a moment how much work you should do as an individual investor in selecting the securities you are considering for purchase. First, you should become familiar with the industry that the company is involved in and research how well-positioned it is compared with its peers and whether it has competitive advantage. This alone will not lead to success, thus you must be prepared to make an assessment of the quality of the management team running the company, which can be done by looking at their previous history, or perhaps the companies that they used to work for, and whether they were well-run.

Do not invest in a stock without first examining the company's financials, which is a shorthand way of referring to the financial statements companies issue every three months. These offer detail on their income and expenses, profits and losses, and their equity value and debts. Learning to understand company statements is a task in itself, but you must be able to assess the company's financial position from their latest statement in order to feel confident when investing your money.

Finally, if you have determined that a company is worthy of your investment, this still does not cover the question of how the rest of the market regards the company. Remember that the share price depends not just on the actual company — the company has no direct cash connection to the price — but on how the market as a whole views the company. The price rises or falls according to investor sentiment, and supply and demand. If a company pays a dividend, that is the only real monetary connection to the shareholder.

So you may decide to defer to the manager's expertise in selecting which shares or bonds the fund invests in. You can be confident that the manager will apply expertise to the task at hand to make the best selections; he or she will work hard to ensure that funds perform well. Managers are aware that there are many thousands of mutual funds available to investors and are eagerly striving to be in the list of the top 10 or top 20 performing funds so that more investors seek their services and buy into their fund.

In the chapter on fund selection, I note that previous performance is only one factor to be considered, as it is seldom that the best-performing fund in any particular sector remains this way year after year. However, many would-be investors place great weight in how well the funds performed last year, and the more new clients the manager can attract to the fund, the better placed a manager is to demand a better salary and benefits. Incidentally, in these days of job losses, excellent fund performance is also the manager's assurance that he or she is unlikely to be laid off.

No matter how well you believe you understand the market, it is unlikely that you have the time to commit that the manager has. If you can select the securities to invest in better than the manager, then it may be that you are in the wrong line of work. Many investors fancy themselves as armchair quarterbacks but, in practice, they would likely find a manager's job overwhelming.

In the case of a massive decline in the market, such as the 40 percent drop at the end of 2008, you may find that you are protected to some extent with a full-time manager. After all, if you have your own independent investment portfolio and are not following it closely — perhaps you are on holiday — you would be fully suffering the losses that happened.

On the other hand, your fund manager may take steps to protect your investment, perhaps selling and moving into cash temporarily, when he or she sees that the problem is looming.

Diversification

Another mutual fund feature that is difficult to emulate independently is the diversification available. When you select a mutual fund, it will often concentrate on a particular type of investment, such as bonds or stocks, and many funds will narrow this selection further by looking for a large-cap growth, small international value, or other combinations. Thus, you can finish with a specialized mutual fund investment.

Even so, given the resources available for investing in a well-supported mutual fund, managers are easily able to diversify between the choices of stocks or bonds to hedge their selection against any unfortunate news affecting one of the companies. Unless you have considerable funds to invest, it would likely be impractical for you to take on shares of as many different companies as the fund can.

Though diversification cannot protect you completely from a market slump — such was recently experienced where the shares of virtually all the companies listed on the stock exchange suffered a drastic reduction in value — it performs well when bad news about a company or a contract emerges that affects a particular stock. In such a situation, you might expect a typical mutual fund to be affected by only 1 or 2 percent, even if the stock suffered a sharp decline.

Incremental Saving

Another advantage of investing in a mutual fund is not needing to have a large sum of money all at once. Mutual fund shares are not expensive, and buying a few gives you the advantage of investing in all the companies that the fund has in its portfolio. There is often a minimum that the fund will accept to open the account, but this gives you the same access to the companies' returns as any investor.

In addition, it can be an ideal way to commit to regular savings. Many mutual funds allow you to make regular monthly payments directly from your bank account, which will increase your shareholdings steadily. If you were to invest in shares on your own, this would be a different proposition and would require you to make choices as to which companies you wanted to invest in on which months.

Although many advocate a money market-based fund if you want access to your money in a short time, mutual funds have the advantage of liquidity. This is one of many regulations governing mutual funds and separating them from other investment opportunities, such as hedge funds. Mutual funds are required to calculate their NAV every day, and shares can be easily redeemed as necessary for your financial requirements.

Many advisors do not recommend a share-based mutual fund for money that you might need to cover unforeseen bills because the NAV will vary with the share price and the stock market, and Murphy's Law dictates that when you want your money, the stock market will have a dip in its prices. Outside of this consideration, the liquidity aspect applies to any type of mutual fund, which makes these funds an accessible form of investment.

Other Choices

An alternative investment strategy to a mutual fund is to find a full-service stockbroker who can provide you with recommendations of stocks that he or she believes will perform well. Some conflict of interest can be present here, as the stockbroker may charge a commission for each transaction that he or she did on your behalf, and it can be in the interests of the stockbroker to trade more than necessary in order to achieve high commissions.

Another increasingly popular broker variety is the Web site-based broker, in which you make your own stock selections and enter the trades at a low cost, typically $7-$10. With careful mutual fund selection, you can buy and sell shares in the fund with no load and no charges; thus, you will have eliminated the brokers' fees associated with individual investment.

If you wish to invest your money in a relatively safe place, you may consider buying bank CDs or opening a savings account. The advantage of using a mutual fund instead is that the rate of return, even with a mutual fund selected to carry low risk, is likely to be better than what you can achieve with customary bank investments. You can find funds that also have added advantages, similar to those you can get from a bank, such as being able to write checks on the account.

Most mutual funds will allow you to use the Internet or phone to arrange a funds transfer to your bank. However, if you have a money-market mutual fund, you can treat this as cash in a similar way to your bank account. You will frequently be able to get a check book, which is an ideal way to save your emergency funds and earn a good rate of return. You may still need to keep a bank account for regular small bills, as the checking that you have on your money market account will likely have a minimum amount required for each check you write. This may be a few hundred dollars, ensuring that the mutual fund does not have the high staffing costs of dealing with many small amounts.

CHAPTER 8

What is the Downside?

With many advantages in using mutual funds for your investment portfolio, some investors might wonder why they should consider anything else. Provided you have a reasonable spread to give you proper diversification across the different markets, a mutual fund portfolio can make good sense. However, there are factors involved with mutual funds that could be considered disadvantages.

Expenses

One issue is that you are incurring costs and fees for the privilege of holding mutual funds. You might be paying for the privilege of buying or even selling them. If you are prepared to do your homework regarding what sectors of the marketplace in what proportions you should invest in, consider why you should pay fees for someone to emulate your work.

The answer to this depends on your personality. The fact that someone else is handling your money day-to-day is also listed as an advantage, but the disadvantage is that the more money taken out in expenses, the less you have accumulating with compound returns. The effect of this should not be underestimated.

As an example, say you held a mutual fund in stocks that averaged a 10 percent return before expenses, but expenses were 2 percent. If you held $100,000 in this fund for 20 years, you would have nearly $470,000 at the end of this time. That is $100,000 compounded at 8 percent, and half a million dollars is an excellent return. However, if you are prepared to do your homework and research the stocks — or follow the fund and buy the stocks that the fund buys, selling when the fund sells — your return could be 10 percent and, after 20 years, your $100,000 could become worth more than $670,000.

Lack of Control

Another disadvantage is the lack of control you may feel by not having direct involvement in where your money is being invested. You may follow the stock market to some extent, or perhaps you just read feature articles in the newspaper on particular companies, and reviewing your funds' holdings may cause you to consider that you could do a better job. This feeling particularly can feel like an issue when the markets are down and your mutual fund may be "in the red" for the year. You must consider whether you could deal with this feeling without deciding to abandon your investment strategy.

You may be aware that the Federal Deposit Insurance Corporation (FDIC) provides insurance to customers of banks, which means even if the bank runs out of money through circumstances or mis-management, you will be able to claim back up to $100,000 of the money you have deposited there. This amount is even higher in some cases, such as if the deposit is in a retirement fund.

This gives many people some reassurance, particularly those who are wary of anyone else looking after their business. The high-street banks that are included in this scheme contribute to the FDIC each year in what is in essentially an insurance premium to cover your money. With the larger bankruptcies, such as Indy-Mac in 2008, there has been some concern that the FDIC may run out of money to cover all contingencies, and it does appear they might need to increase the premiums charged, given the credit meltdown and its effect on financial institutions.

If the FDIC does run out of money because of the fundamen-tal purpose of their mission, I have little doubt that the federal government will bail them out as much as necessary. This means that, provided you are careful how much money you put in each bank, your savings are protected from loss.

However, this is not the case when you put your money into a mutual fund. There is no FDIC insurance for a mutual fund and, therefore, the investment company facilitating that fund could, in theory, go bankrupt without insurance protection.

But this lack of insurance is not the disadvantage of investing in mutual funds that it may appear to be. Even if the invest-ment company is not good at managing its own accounts, your investment is actually in the bonds and the stocks that the fund holds, so your main risk of losing your money depends on these stocks and bonds — not on who is overseeing the investment. Mutual funds are heavily regulated and should not be subject to some of the manipulations we have seen in other financial areas.

For example, you may have heard about hedge funds and the issues they have experienced in the recent financial collapse. Indeed, mutual funds are not immune to the effects of the financial market, and their performance has been drastically curtailed during this current the credit crisis. However, if you are concerned that mutual funds have no FDIC protection, consider that the high street bank typically holds less than 20 cents for every dollar that has been invested because its business is lending out that money at a higher rate of interest. The mutual fund, in contrast, holds actual assets, such as shares, thus money is not lost, though values can vary. The shares are not even held by the mutual fund in a way that they can be interfered with; they are instead held by a separate organization that keeps safe custody of them.

Although the NAV must be calculated daily because of the regulations controlling mutual funds, that does not mean that you know how much you will receive when you sell your shares in the mutual fund. The NAV is often determined after all exchanges have closed — which is a sensible choice, as the share prices that comprise he fund will be fixed until the next market opening — and you may instruct the fund during the day that you want to redeem some shares. There is no way that you will know how much you will receive for them until the markets have closed and the NAV has been calculated.

This may seem to be a disadvantage to you if you are used to the way that company shares are bought and sold. When you call your stockbroker or log in online, you are presented with the current price and can decide on the basis of that firm information on whether you wish to buy or sell any shares. If you are buying shares online, you may find you pay even less than the price that was shown on your screen. Brokers are required to fill your order in the best possible way, which may mean that they find a slightly cheaper source of the stocks when you place your order.

If you are not careful with your fund selection, you may find that you are buying yourself into a disadvantage with some funds. Despite what has been said about diversification, you should be aware that there are some mutual funds, particularly ones special-izing in certain sectors, that would not be considered adequately diversified against particular market trends. These mutual funds are designed to be part of a balanced portfolio or to direct the investment of someone who is prepared to follow sector trends and does not mind taking the risks associated with betting on one particular side. These specialized funds are also the ones that seem to have higher operating expenses, which is another disad-vantage to using them, unless the particular sector is considered important to your strategy.

Possible Inconvenience

If you are looking to keep your emergency funds in a money market mutual fund rather than a bank account, you may find it a disadvantage that you have minimum amount restrictions on your check-writing facilities. You will likely have to maintain an account at your local bank for smaller checks. For day-to-day expenses, the convenience of an ATM at the bank cannot be matched by a mutual fund account.

For some, the idea of placing your funds somewhere that you likely must send mail to — rather than somewhere you can physically walk into — may be a problem. Mutual fund offices do exist, but not to anywhere near the same extent as bank branches, and because you will want to select one of the better mutual funds, it is likely that the head office of the particular fund you choose is located a distance from where you live.

Be careful when selecting mutual funds so you do not include any that invest in derivatives unless you understand the logic behind this philosophy. Derivatives are financial manipulations designed to multiply the effect of your money; for example, if a stock goes up $1, you may gain $3. Of course, the opposite applies, and if you choose the wrong side of the transaction, you may lose more than it cost you. Such mutual funds should reveal their basis in the prospectus, and exposing your investment to this degree of riskiness might be something you consider a disadvantage.

Having said that, it is possible to use derivatives in combination with your holdings in order to hedge the investment against an unfortunate price move. If the fund states that derivatives are used for this purpose and specifically explains how, then you may find it acceptable.

Tax issues are touched on in a later chapter, though for detailed advice, you should obtain your own accountant — unless you feel competent enough to wade through the forms offered by the IRS. The tax treatment of mutual funds can be more elaborate than with other investments because the money that you make on the funds can be counted in various ways, depending on its source.

Some of the money that a mutual fund makes, assuming that it increases its value, will come from dividends paid on the stocks that it holds. Other money that the fund makes includes buying and selling stocks at a profit, and if the stocks have been held for less than a year, this money is subject to a different tax treatment. This money is classified as short-term capital gains, and it is normally taxed at your ordinary income tax rate. You will receive a regular dividend from the mutual fund, which will be declared to you on a Form 1099-DIV for tax purposes and, as a rule, you will not pay capital gains on a mutual fund holding until you sell it.

CASE STUDY: KEITH NEWCOMB

Keith Newcomb is an adviser with 12 years' experience helping people align their finances and investments with achieving life's goals. His insights have been sought by publications including *The Wall Street Journal®*, *Business Week*, *Financial Times*, *Investor's Business Daily*, *AARP® Bulletin®*, *Money magazine*, *Kiplinger's®*, *Reader's Digest*, the *Journal of Financial Planning*, and many financial industry trade publications. He is also active in the leadership of the Financial Planning Association, a 29,000-member trade association, serving in 2009 as Chairman of the Government Relations Committee and as a member of the board of directors of the FPA-PAC.

He is the founder of wealth management firm Full Life Financial LLC, a registered investment adviser.

For more information, go to: **www.KeithNewcomb.com**

How did you get into the field of mutual fund investments?

I began by seeking out personal investments, before becoming a professional adviser.

As an investment adviser, what do you see as your primary function when selecting investments?

Understanding your goals and bringing clarity to the plan for achieving them is paramount. Investment selection flows from understanding and clarity.

Given the current state of the financial markets, have you changed the way that you select any investments, or is your existing strategy already coping well?

Investment selection is only half the strategy. The other half is de-selection. A disciplined, flexible approach to both buying and selling is helpful in any market environment.

CASE STUDY: KEITH NEWCOMB

What do you like and dislike about mutual funds?

I like specialized professional management in niches, the diversification inherent in funds, and view no-load or load-waived mutual funds as an asset allocation tool. I am less enthused by the limitations of end-of-day pricing, unfavorable tax treatment of income and capital gain distributions, the impact on fund managers of having to manage around inflows and outflows, and the layers of expenses involved (from sales charges, to management fees, 12(b)-1 fees, embedded soft dollar costs and trading commissions, and tax consequences of embedded gains and losses in established portfolios). The ETF structure holds promise as a way funds can overcome some of these problems. I think mutual funds may gravitate toward offering their existing strategies in an ETF vehicle in the future.

What personal qualities do you think help you succeed as an investment adviser?

The ability to understand people and bring clarity to their finances and investments. I am told that is an unusual combination. It probably helps the folks I work with feel a sense of comfort and trust in our advice. From my perspective as a professional adviser, that's the key to being able to do the right thing for our clients.

What is the biggest success you have had concerning mutual funds?

Realizing that you can never stop learning how to continuously improve your portfolio management process — there will never be a single biggest success. Rather, consistently seeking improvement is success.

What is the biggest challenge that you have had to face?

I love my clients, and I love my work. Finding "me time" is a constant challenge.

What advice would you give to potential investors, particularly in the face of the economic crisis, and how would this vary depending on their age?

Simplify. Work with a professional you are comfortable with and a firm in which you trust. Follow the advice you pay for. If you find that too hard to swallow and you need to make a change in adviser(s), go ahead. When you do, start by

CASE STUDY: KEITH NEWCOMB

understanding what you want to accomplish, the resources you have in terms of time and money, and the risks that might disrupt your progress, and both your financial capacity and personal preferences with respect to handling those risks. These steps are important because they provide a context for investment selection.

You asked about age. I think age is relative, and the same number might mean different things to different people. The overall context of your life situation is much more important than your chronological age. Clearly match your investment strategies to your time horizon for each goal. That means generally reducing risk as the goal date approaches. Carry adequate reserves and insurance to weather surprises. Now more than ever, paying down debt as fast as you can is the surest investment you can make in your future. Adopt a flexible strategy that includes both a buy and sell discipline. Plan, execute, monitor, and adjust.

CHAPTER 9

Who Are The Companies?

Hundreds of investment companies exist in the market, and thousands of funds are available. You could even start your own investment company and sell shares in your own mutual fund; all you must do is acquaint yourself and comply with the laws governing the way you conduct your business. Thus, the number of companies in existence — all of which are vying for your attention — should not be surprising.

In simple terms, a group of investors with a common interest or philosophy will place their money with a company that seems to support their views, and that appears to have the best possibility of a high return. An experienced investment manager and a team of researchers can manage the portfolio, and the staff can study forecasts, domestic and international conditions, company reports, and other variables. The manager then implements his or her recommendations by buying and selling shares and securities.

In essence, that is the way many investment companies are set up. But there are variations to this theme. For example, some funds have a single manager who takes sole responsibility for the day-to-day operation of the fund and all its investment decisions. If these managers are effective, they become well-known in the industry. The danger in such a fund is that the manager may leave or have an accident, and the nature and success of the fund may suffer. There will be other staff in the manager's department, and he or she may indeed discuss selections and actions with colleagues on an unofficial basis, but the manager is ultimately the person responsible for the fund.

Fund companies that are diversified into other areas, such as personal investment advice, retirement accounts, or tax issues, may choose to take the course of appointing another experienced company as an advisor for their fund. Such advisors may work for several fund companies, depending on the closeness of the relationship. This relieves the fund company from needing to set up and maintain a research department and, with careful selection of the advisor, this method can offer positive results. The advisor is immersed in the investments and the market and likely will be an experienced expert.

A different approach that has been adopted by companies such as American Century is to have a management team comprising co-managers who work together and come to agreement on the portfolio at any particular time. Some preferences are revealed occasionally; for example, one manager may specialize in a particular area and have the final say on stock holdings in that specialty, but the idea is that the managers are on equal footing and design the fund by committee.

A few of the mutual fund companies use what is termed a "multiple manager system of administration." This differs from the management team approach in that each manager is responsible for his or her section of the fund and its investments. The managers work independently, and there may even be advisors hired from different investment groups to take care of different aspects in the fund. Thus, this system is the opposite of the team approach. An example of this type of fund is the Masters Select.

As for which type of management system produces the best results, there is no clear preference in the performance figures. Perhaps this is no surprise, as it will be the quality of the managers' selections that will be reflected in the fund's performance, regardless of which system the fund company is organized under. This explains why so many different management structures can exist, as there is no general move toward any one of them as the superior system.

Some companies are still limited in their scope, though I have ensured that the companies I have listed are established with a reasonable amount of existing investment. Some investment advisor firms set up their own funds for their clients to invest in, and some companies approach mutual fund management from the other direction by specializing in the mutual funds and not necessarily offering any individual advice to potential investors, but merely being as informative as they can in the literature describing their funds, such as the prospectus described in the next chapter.

For convenience, I have listed a number of companies and arranged them alphabetically with their Web site addresses and the types of funds they feature. The list is extensive but by no means comprehensive, and it is not meant to imply that any fund companies not listed are not worthy of consideration.

For the particularly well-known fund companies, I have included additional details about their background. Where I have not, please refer to the companies' Web sites if you are interested in knowing more. Most of the Web sites will give you the performance figures of the funds, but I suggest that you refer to these for confirmation once you have short-listed the funds you are interested in. For your initial search, use one of the independent online services mentioned in the next chapter for your initial filter.

1st Source Bank

www.1stsource.com

Offers an income equity fund, an income fund, and a long/short fund.

Activa Mutual Funds

www.activafunds.com

Presents an intermediate bond fund; a value fund, which is a large-cap fund; a growth fund; and an international fund.

Adams Express Company

www.adamsexpress.com

A conservative closed-end fund with the distinction of being nearly 80 years old and paying dividends for the last 74 years.

AdvisorOne Funds

www.advisoronefunds.com

Amerigo is the name of a large-cap fund. They also have Clermont, Berolina, Descartes, another large-cap fund, and Liahona.

Aegis Value

www.aegisfunds.com

Aegis Value Fund concentrates on small company stocks that appear to be undervalued. The aim is to invest in economical companies that have a good prospect of appreciation.

Aegis also runs a high-yield fund that has been in existence about five years. This concentrates on high-yield or junk bonds, which means it is riskier than some funds, but it is also no-load and high-yielding.

AIM

www.aiminvestments.com

Invesco Aim has a selection of financial products and mutual funds in all shapes and sizes. Their Web site gives a complete rundown of the financial figures and the aims and goals of each fund.

AIP

www.aipfunds.com

AIP run two mutual funds, which are different from the normal funds. They boast of hedge fund strategies in a mutual fund, which means they are intended to produce higher returns with a corresponding high risk. As such, they also have higher operating expenses.

Al Frank

www.alfrank.com

Al Frank Funds concentrate on buying undervalued securities. The Al Frank Fund has been in existence more than 10 years, and within the last five years, they have also introduced a dividend value fund.

Alpine Funds

www.alpinefunds.com

Alpine Funds have a selection of ten different funds and are a good place to look for fixed income and real-estate-based funds, as they have several to choose from.

Amana Mutual Funds Trust

www.amanafunds.com

They have a growth fund and an income fund, both of which are large-cap stocks based.

American Beacon

www.americanbeaconfunds.com

This company has a wide range of funds in most market sectors.

American Century Investments

www.americancentury.com

Another company with a diverse range of funds, including stock funds, bond funds, assets allocation funds, and money market funds.

Ameristock Funds

www.ameristock.com

The Ameristock mutual fund is large-cap based.

AMF Asset Management Fund

www.amffunds.com

They have a large-cap equity fund, as well as some bond and money market funds.

Arbitrage

www.thearbfund.com

The Arbitrage Funds have a steady performance, even during this economic crisis, which may result from their approach to the market. The goal is to achieve capital growth, primarily from mergers and acquisitions arbitrage. As such, these are unusual funds and are not easily categorized.

Ariel Mutual Funds

www.arielmutualfunds.com

Ariel has just three funds, all of them value, covering a range of equity size.

Artisan Funds

www.artisanfunds.com

Artisan Funds offer a small range of ten funds covering small, medium, large cap, international, growth, and value. The company was founded in 1994 and has about $30 billion in managed assets, which includes mutual funds and separate account management.

Their international value fund, specializing in foreign small and mid-cap companies, achieved a five-star rating with Morningstar, and their domestic mid-cap and small-cap funds are both well-regarded.

AssetMark

www.assetmark.com

AssetMark funds are a family of mutual funds and have recently merged with Genworth Financial, which provides general financial services and advice. Their minimum investment is $50,000.

Aston Funds

www.astonfunds.com

Aston has 26 no-load mutual funds in various classes.

Auxier Asset Management LLC

www.auxierasset.com

The Auxier Focus fund concentrates on large-cap stocks.

Ave Maria

www.avemariafund.com

There are five different Ave Maria funds and a money market account, run by Schwartz Investment Counsel Inc., which is a registered investment advisor with its own fund. The emphasis is on moral responsibility as well as sound investment, and they choose companies that do not violate Catholic teachings.

The Catholic Advisory Board is responsible for setting out the values that conform to their standards and, specifically, are pro-life and pro-family, avoiding anything related to abortion, pornography, and the undermining of family values.

Baron Funds

www.baronfunds.com

Baron invests in small-cap, medium-cap, and large-cap companies for growth, with a family of eight funds.

Becker Capital Management Inc.

www.beckercap.com

Becker has a value-equity fund, investing in large-cap stocks.

Berwyn

www.berwynfunds.com

Berwyn provides three mutual funds. Started 25 years ago, it has two value offerings and an income fund.

Biondo Investment Advisors

www.thebiondogroup.com

This growth fund invests in large-cap stocks.

Brandywine Funds

www.brandywinefunds.com

Managed by Friess Associates, Brandywine has three funds, including Brandywine Blue, a large-cap stock fund.

Bridges Investment Management

www.bridgesinv.com

Bridges offers growth and income funds based on large-cap stocks.

Bridgeway Funds

www.bridgeway.com

This company has a family of 11 funds, including small and large growth and value.

Buffalo Funds

www.buffalofunds.com

Buffalo has a family of ten funds, covering different sectors and sizes.

Caldwell & Orkin

www.caldwellorkin.com

Caldwell & Orkin have a "Market Opportunity Fund," which uses aggressive investment strategies to try to achieve high returns. Their strategies, including short selling and options, are spelled out in detail in their prospectus.

California Investment Trust

www.caltrust.com

This no-load mutual fund company has 12 funds, which cover every primary asset class.

Cambiar Investors

www.cambiar.com

Cambiar funds cover just-for-asset classes, including large-cap, small cap, international equity, and global multi-cap.

CGM Funds

www.cgmfunds.com

The CGM mutual fund aims for capital appreciation and has 75 percent stock and 25 percent debt or equity distribution.

Chase Investment Counsel

www.chaseinv.com

Chase has three open-end, no-load growth funds, one of which has a minimum $1,000,000 investment.

Clipper Fund

www.clipperfund.com

The Clipper fund is a large-cap, stock-based, no-load mutual fund.

Columbia Management

www.columbiafunds.com

This family of funds spans nearly every asset class and level of risk, with a wide selection of funds to choose from.

Country Financial

www.countryfinancial.com

Country offers 11 funds, which cover the range of the marketplace.

CRM

www.crmfunds.com

Cramer Rosenthal McGlynn (CRM) now operates two mutual funds after adding two funds in 2008 with an international perspective.

Cullen Funds

www.cullenfunds.com

Cullen has two funds, one domestic and one international, with both characterized as high dividend.

Davenport & Company

www.davenportllc.com

Davenport & Company LLC is an investment advisor offering an equity fund based on large-cap stocks.

Direxion

www.direxionfunds.com

Offering two funds in high-yield bonds, one of them designed for a bear market.

Dreyfus

www.dreyfus.com

Dreyfus provides a comprehensive number of funds, covering a diverse range of sectors and sizes.

DWS Investments

www.dws-investments.com

The list of mutual funds that this company provides is also quite comprehensive, giving you a wide selection.

Elite Mutual Funds

www.elitefunds.com

These funds are managed by McCormick Capital Management and include an income fund.

Embarcadero Funds

www.embarcaderomutualfunds.com

Embarcadero Funds (formerly Van Wagoner) claim better-than-average performance for their family of equity funds. They have a small-cap, an all-cap, and an alternative strategies fund, which invests in other mutual funds to achieve low correlation to the markets.

Fairholme Fund

www.fairholmefunds.com

The Fairholme fund has historically performed consistently better than the S&P 500.

FAM Funds

www.famfunds.com

Fenimore Asset Management is a company of professional investment managers with two FAM mutual funds of its own, a value fund, and an equity-income fund.

FBR

www.fbrfunds.com

FBR Capital Markets is another network of advisors that has ten mutual funds, including a few sector offerings.

Federated

www.federatedinvestors.com

Federated are investment managers who give access to 158 different mutual funds. They deal in a variety of funds, including closed-end municipal funds.

Fidelity

www.fidelity.com

One of the major players in the investment industry, Fidelity has 175 no-load funds available with more than 300 total funds. They also provide access from their Web site to thousands of other funds from leading fund companies, and also have a fund evaluator to discourage you from straying for your mutual fund needs.

Though known as a mutual fund company, they offer a variety of advice for retirement, estate planning, and more. They trace their roots back to the 1940s; in 1946, they reported $13 million in assets management. They are now the largest mutual fund company in America in terms of the assets they control.

Fiduciary Management Inc.

www.fiduciarymgt.com

FMI, as they prefer to be called, has been in the business since 1980 and offers four different funds.

First Eagle Fund

www.firsteaglefunds.com

The First Eagle family of funds comprises only five funds, but these are claimed to be fully complimentary. They include domestic and overseas offerings, as well as a gold fund.

Flippin, Bruce, & Porter

www.fbpinc.com

These investment counselors operate two mutual funds, a value fund, and a balanced fund.

FMA

www.fmausa.com

Fiduciary Management Associates LLC is an investment management company with four fund products, including a fixed-income fund.

Forward

www.forwardfunds.com

Forward Funds have 12 mutual funds that, in addition to the normal range, include a real estate and an emerging-market fund.

Franklin Templeton Investments

www.franklintempleton.com

Franklin Templeton offer a large number of mutual funds. The greatest number is known as the Franklin family, and there are also Franklin Templeton funds, Mutual Series funds, and Templeton funds.

Gabelli

www.gabelli.com

Also known as GAMCO Investors Inc., Gabelli has a comprehensive set of mutual funds, as well as other financial products. They feature fixed income, open-end — both with and without loads — money market, and closed-end funds.

GKM Advisers

www.gkmadvisers.com

They have a growth fund that emphasizes low turnover in its holdings.

Guinness Atkinson

www.gafunds.com

A different approach is taken by Guinness Atkinson, who have created a fund portfolio specifically aimed at profiting from global change; to this end, their six funds are concentrated on investing in energy and Asian markets.

Harbor Funds

www.harborfunds.com

Harbor Funds have a variety of no-load funds available, covering growth, value, and fixed income, both in the U.S. and internationally. They have a total of 27 different offerings in mutual funds and also manage pension plans. The total funds in management are about $33 million.

Heartland Funds

www.heartlandfunds.com

Heartland concentrates on finding stocks that are undervalued. All three of their funds are value funds.

Hennessy Funds

www.hennessyfunds.com

Hennessy offers six different stock-based funds.

Henssler Financial Group

www.henssler.com

Henssler concentrates on providing one no-load, high-quality stock fund, with an emphasis on selecting for growth.

HighMark Funds

www.highmarkfunds.com

HighMark has a family of 24 funds, including money market and fixed income, and provides one place to buy a diversified portfolio.

Hillman Capital Management

www.hillmancapital.com

Hillman Capital offers eight different equity funds. While not as diverse as some of the other companies, they do offer a good selection.

Hodges Fund

www.hodgesfund.com

Hodges have major funds, including all sizes of company, as well as a small-cap fund.

Holland Capital Management

www.hollandcap.com

The Lou Holland Growth Fund is available from Schwab and Fidelity.

Homestead Funds

www.homesteadfunds.com

Homestead has eight funds and includes a variety, such as shares, bonds, government, small, and international.

Hussman Funds

www.hussmanfunds.com

Dr. Hussman runs two funds as President of Hussman Funds. The Strategic Growth Fund concentrates on long-term capital growth, while the Total Return Fund includes government securities and emphasizes long-term returns.

Icon Funds

www.iconadvisers.com

They feature a range of funds, but with a manageable number. Icon covers different sectors and different areas of the world.

IMS

www.imscapital.com

IMS Capital Management has several offices and has been in existence more than 20 years. Their three funds are available from several other mutual fund platforms.

ING Mutual Funds

www.ingfunds.com

One of the major companies; you are likely familiar with ING from their extensive advertising. They have both open-end and closed-end funds, as well as other varieties.

James Advantage Funds

www.jamesfunds.com

James Investment Research manages these funds and has been in the business since 1972. There are five funds, ranging from conservative to the more risky small-cap and short-selling types.

Janus

www.janus.com

Although not as large as some, Janus is another major company providing many varieties of funds.

Jensen Investment Management

www.jenseninvestment.com

Like other companies in the financial world that do not have a range of funds, Jensen is an asset management firm. Many such companies prefer creating their own product, thus Jensen has its own mutual fund, called the Jensen Portfolio.

Kalmar

www.kalmarinvestments.com

Kalmar focuses on growth with value and has a preponderance of small-cap companies in their fund, which was created in 1997.

Kinetics Mutual Funds

www.kineticsfunds.com

Kinetics has a small number of funds and focuses on particular themes, such as water, the Internet, and health care.

Laudus

www.laudusfunds.com

Laudus offers three "flavors" of fund: their Laudus Rosenberg, Laudus Mondrian, and Laudus MarketMasters ranges. The first is sub-advised by AXA Rosenberg and offers nine funds. The second is a smaller set of four funds, advised by Mondrian Investment Partners.

The MarketMasters range uses a multi-manager hierarchy for three all-embracing funds, and the total funds under management exceed $3.5 billion.

Lazard

www.lazardnet.com

Lazard offers 12 open-end funds, which cater to many different types of investing.

Leavell Investment Management

www.tleavell.com

As an investment advisor, T. Leavell & Associates Inc. manages three no-load funds, called Government Street Funds.

Longleaf Partners

www.longleafpartners.com

Longleaf Partners funds actively discourage investment from market timers, according to their Web site. They have three funds, all value-based, covering the larger companies, smaller companies, and international opportunities.

Loomis Sayles

www.loomissayles.com

Loomis Sayles has been offering financial advice for more than 80 years. They offer a range of income, growth, and value funds, both with and without loads.

Luther King Capital Management

www.lkcm.com

This financial firm is associated with LKCM Funds and the LKCM Aquinas Funds. This latter is a group of four funds that seek to promote Catholic values, and the former has five funds in general areas.

Madison Mosaic Funds

www.mosaicfunds.com

A mid-size fund company, Mosaic offers five stock funds, three bond funds, two tax-free funds, and a money market fund. The total of 11 funds covers a good range of the marketplace.

Mairs and Power Funds

www.mairsandpower.com

The investment advisers offer two funds to the public: a growth fund and a balanced fund.

Managers Investment Group

www.managersinvest.com

Managers offers a wide array of funds covering many of the asset classes. They divide their funds into Managers Funds and Managers AMG Funds for further variety.

Manning & Napier Advisors Inc.

www.manningnapieradvisors.com

They have a number of funds, covering domestic and foreign stocks, and taxable and tax-free bonds.

Markman Capital

www.markman.com

Markman specializes in a core-growth fund, which they claim adapts to changing market conditions. They also have a global fund.

Marshall Funds

www.marshallfunds.com

Marshall funds are also known as M & I and have a range of 17 funds, including equities, fixed-income, and money market funds.

Marsico Funds

www.marsicofunds.com

Marsico has six different funds available, which include international offerings. According to the Web site, they all seek long-term growth of capital.

Masters' Select Funds

www.mastersselect.com

Masters', under Litman/Gregory Fund Advisors LLC, identifies managers who are committed to a small number of stocks, believing that this focuses the manager's talents. However, they diversify the funds by using several managers for each. They have five funds, including international and small-cap.

This policy is based on the beliefs of Litman/Gregory fund advisors, who are the investment advisers for Masters' Select.

Matrix Advisors Value Fund

www.matrixadvisorsvaluefund.com

Matrix advisors is a stock portfolio manager that decided to create a mutual fund in line with their philosophies.

Matthew 25

www.matthew25fund.com

A single fund: an open-end, no-load growth and value fund that is designed for capital appreciation, not income.

Meridian Fund Inc.

www.meridianfund.com

Meridian started in 1984 with a growth fund and has added a value fund and an equity income fund since then. They have been ranked highly in the press.

Metropolitan West

www.mwamllc.com

Metropolitan West, or MetWest, offers a selection of funds mainly centered on bonds. They concentrate on capital preservation and fixed income.

Monetta Mutual Funds

www.monetta.com

Monetta has a family of five funds, covering a range of needs.

Muhlenkamp & Company Inc.

www.muhlenkamp.com

Muhlenkamp is an independent investment management firm that has set up a mutual fund.

Needham

www.needhamfunds.com

Needham Mutual Funds include three distinct types of growth fund — an aggressive growth, a long-term growth, and a small-cap growth. They are all open-end and no-load funds.

Neuberger Berman

www.nb.com

This company was founded in 1939 and started offering mutual funds in 1950, claiming a great deal of corporate experience in asset management. They offer equity funds, closed-end funds, fixed-income funds, and variable annuities for institutional clients.

New Century Portfolios

www.newcenturyportfolios.com

New Century has six funds, including a money market fund and an international fund. Five concentrate on capital growth, and the Balanced fund has a principal purpose of earning income.

New Covenant Mutual Funds

www.newcovenantfunds.com

New Covenant offers a variety in five funds, including growth and income. They advocate socially responsible investing, as part of the Presbyterian Foundation Group.

New River

www.newriverfunds.com

Known as SouthernSun Funds, they have a small-cap capital appreciation fund.

Nicholas Company Inc.

www.nicholasfunds.com

Nicolas is one of the older investment companies, founded in 1967. It offers seven mutual funds and claims to combine both value and growth strategies in what they call Growth at a Reasonable Price (GARP).

Northeast Investors

www.northeastinvestors.com

Northeast has two funds: a high-yield bond fund and a large-cap growth-stocks fund.

Northern Funds

www.northernfunds.com

Northern Funds has been in investment management since 1889 and manages more than $750 billion. They have a substantial list of mutual funds and a great variety in market and risk.

Oak Associates Funds

www.oakfunds.com

Oak Associates has seven mutual funds, all with the word "oak" in their names, covering fields such as emerging technologies and health.

Oak Value Fund

www.oakvaluefund.com

Oak concentrates on high-value large-cap companies for their single mutual fund offering.

Oberweis

www.oberweisfunds.com

Oberweis has six mutual funds and specializes in small-cap investing for the anticipated high growth potential. They include Asia in their portfolio.

Old Mutual Capital

www.oldmutualfunds.com

Old Mutual started in 1845 in South Africa and has more than $500 billion in managed assets. They have a significant number of mutual funds in all categories and markets.

Olstein

www.olsteinfunds.com

Olsten recently announced their second fund, which invests in strategic opportunities. Their first fund has been renamed All Cap Value.

Optique Funds

www.optiquefunds.com

This is a new company established at the end of 2007, though the management team has much experience. They offer four funds at the moment: a large-cap, a small-cap, an international, and a fixed-income fund.

Osterweis

www.osterweis.com

Osterweis Capital Management, in addition to individually managing accounts, runs two mutual funds: a fixed-income and an equity fund for long-term appreciation.

Paradigm

www.paradigm-funds.com

Paradigm Funds has four offerings, each of which claims to seek long-term capital appreciation, albeit by investing in different ways.

Parnassus Investments

www.parnassus.com

Parnassus has six no-load mutual funds available, covering the general categories of small, neat, large-cap, and fixed-income, as well as two others based on company characteristics.

Pax World Investments

www.paxworld.com

Pax World Mutual Funds claim to be in support of sustainable investing. They look for companies that are socially responsible, in addition to meeting financial standards. Besides the general varieties, they have a Global Green Fund, which looks for companies that help mitigate the global impact of commerce, and a Women's

Equity Fund, which not only has socially responsible choices, but avoids any company associated with weapons or tobacco, and recognizes groups that take affirmative steps to advance equality for women.

Payden & Rygel

www.payden.com

With 24 funds to choose from, there is a high probability you can find what you want with this company. They offer three mutual fund families — Paydenfunds, Metzler/Payden Funds, and Payden/Wilshire Longevity Funds — which are target-date funds.

Permanent Portfolio

www.permanentportfoliofunds.com

The Permanent Portfolio family of funds is designed to grow wealth, and the four funds available combine diversification for risk avoidance with potential for higher rewards.

Perritt

www.perrittmutualfunds.com

Perritt Funds seek to benefit from investing in small firms, otherwise known as micro-cap, which seem to have great potential. Their second fund, the emerging opportunities fund, continues in this vein, looking for small companies that have a high management investment rate and low debt.

Petroleum & Resources Corporation

www.peteres.com

Petroleum & Resources Corporation has a closed-end fund specializing in a conservative approach to the energy sector.

Philadelphia Fund Inc.

www.philadelphiafund.com

Philadelphia Fund is a mutual fund that aims for long-term growth based on large-cap companies.

Pinnacle

www.pinnaclevaluefund.com

Pinnacle is a fund in which the portfolio manager and family have a self-professed significant investment. They look for a sound foundation and ignore stocks.

Presidio

www.presidiofunds.com

The Presidio Fund has a general distribution of sectors, including an emphasis on consumer basics and health care.

PRIMECAP® Odyssey Funds

www.odysseyfunds.com

Odyssey offers three funds: growth, aggressive growth, and stocks. All three aim to give long-term capital appreciation, and they focus three to five years out when selecting the securities.

ProFunds®

www.profunds.com

ProFunds has a large portfolio of funds available and claims to be different from the regular investment company. The Web site warns that these funds are not suitable for all investors because of aggressive investment techniques and frequent exchanges, which may increase expenses and taxes. The funds include a family of index funds called Classic; a range called Ultra that tries to double the index; Inverse ProFunds, to provide the exact inverse of the other two, i.e., for bear market gains; UltraSector, for 150 percent of various sector gains; and some dollar-index, treasury, and money funds.

Prudent Bear

www.prudentbear.com

The Federated Prudent Bear Fund is designed to hedge against a bear market by focusing on short selling and precious metals. A second fund, the Federated Prudent Global Income Fund, is composed so it hedges the investor from a declining dollar using overseas investments.

Rainier

www.rainierfunds.com

Five funds covering the general range of small, mid, and large-cap, as well as income, and balanced funds.

Reynolds Funds

www.reynoldsfunds.com

Reynolds simply has a Blue Chip Growth Fund.

Robeco Investment Management

www.robecoinvest.com

One of Europe's leading investment companies, Robeco offers a wide range of investments.

Royce

www.roycefunds.com

Royce & Associates' investment managers have been around for decades. They have built up their mutual fund offerings from just one in 1972 to 23 open-end and 3 closed-end funds at present, covering a range of risk.

Rydex / SGI

www.rydexfunds.com

Rydex|SGI, formerly Rydex Investments, offers many financial vehicles. Within the mutual fund grouping are multiple index funds as well as sector products, and they also sell exchange-traded funds. They have more than 100 from which to choose and manage more than $12 billion in assets.

Schneider Capital Management

www.schneidercap.com

This employee-owned company has been in operation since 1997. They have a value fund and a small-cap value fund.

Schwab®

www.schwab.com

Charles Schwab is a well-known name in the financial world. While they are involved in many different aspects of investment, including stocks, bonds, options, and CDs, they handle a number of mutual funds and have their own range of more than 50 no-load funds.

Schwartz

www.schwartzinvest.com

In addition to running the Ave Maria Fund, they have their own offering called the Schwartz Value Fund. They look for small- and medium-size companies that appear to favor strong growth.

Scout™ Funds

www.scoutfunds.com

The newly acquired TrendStar Small Cap Fund has been renamed the Scout TrendStar Small Cap Fund. It features an international and small-cap fund, as well as a stock.

Selected Funds

www.selectedfunds.com

Money magazine wrote of Selected Funds, "Sound thinking for a shaky market." They offer three funds: a large-cap, a mid-cap, and a money market fund.

Sentinel Funds

www.sentinelinvestments.com

With 16 funds in all sectors of the market, Sentinel Funds offers one-stop mutual fund shopping.

Sit Mutual Funds

www.sitfunds.com

There are 13 funds in the Sit family, embracing all sizes and types of securities.

Sound Mind Investing Funds

www.smifund.com

Their strategy is to invest in other mutual funds; in other words, they are a fund of funds, and they change the funds invested in when necessary by continuously monitoring which are performing best. They admit they do not try to anticipate which funds are superior, but merely follow and monitor to act swiftly if required.

Their second fund is a Managed Volatility Fund, which has some hedging components built-in to reduce the volatility.

Sound Shore Fund

www.soundshorefund.com

The Sound Shore Fund company has one mutual fund offering: an equity value fund.

SSgA

www.ssgafunds.com

State Street Global Advisors have a number of funds, including index and money market funds. The group is international and has more than $2 trillion u nder management.

Steward Mutual Funds

www.stewardmutualfunds.com

This company offers five mutual funds, which cover most types that one might need.

Stratton Management Company

www.strattonmutualfunds.com

With a motto of "stability, strategy, success," Stratton has a mixed-cap fund, an income fund, and a small-cap value fund.

T. Rowe Price

www.troweprice.com

T. Rowe Price is known as a company of full-service financial advisors. They have more than 90 no-load mutual funds in many areas of investment

TCW

www.tcw.com

TCW has a large range of funds in equities, bonds, and international markets. They cover value and growth in stock funds, and have fixed-income strategies.

TFS Capital®

www.tfscapital.com

TFS has an interactive asset allocation tool on their Web site, which allows you to compare the performance and risk of your current holdings with the TFS Market Neutral Fund. They also have a small-cap fund available, as well as hedge funds for qualified investors.

Third Avenue

www.thirdavenuefunds.com

Third Avenue investment advisors offer a range of four mutual funds, specializing in value, real estate, small-cap, and international market sectors.

Thompson Investment Management Inc.

www.thompsonim.com

Thompson limits their funds to three — a growth fund, a mid-cap fund, and a bond fund. They have only been in operation for a few years in this guise, but the funds originated in 1992.

TIAA-CREF®

www.tiaa-cref.org

These no-load mutual funds have low expense ratios. The company is well-known, covering more than fund management, and they have a number of funds covering most variations that you might require. The company dates back to 1918 and has a strong non-profit heritage.

Tocqueville Mutual Funds

www.tocquevillefunds.com

This company has been managing money for individuals for more than 30 years and has four funds, including a small-cap, an international, and a gold fund.

Torray

www.torray.com

The Torray Fund is a no-load, open-end fund that concentrates on growth over a long period, and it restricts tax liabilities by limiting the realizing of capital gains.

Touchstone Funds

www.touchstonefunds.com

Touchstone concentrates on sub-advised mutual fund solutions. They have a large number of equity, fixed-income, and money market funds.

Transamerica

www.transamerica.com

Transamerica seeks to provide a complete financial package, including life insurance.

Turner Investments

www.turnerinvestments.com

Turner has more than 20 funds available, covering the range of funds that you would need to assemble a complete, diversified portfolio.

Tweedy, Browne Company LLC

www.tweedy.com

Tweedy, Browne has been in the investing business for more than 80 years. They have three mutual funds: the Global Value Fund, the Value Fund, and the Worldwide High Dividend Yield Value Fund.

U.S. Global Investors Inc.

www.usfunds.com

Their family of mutual funds includes six equity funds, three precious metal funds, two tax-free funds, and two money market funds that invest in government securities.

USA Mutuals

www.vicefund.com

USA Mutuals has two distinctive funds. The first, the ViceFund, invests in four sectors for long-term growth — tobacco, alcohol, gaming, and aerospace/defense. The other is called a GenWav-eFund, and it attempts to follow the sectors that will be positively influenced by the baby boomer generation.

USAA

www.usaa.com

USAA provides banking, auto loans, insurance, and many other financial services. They have a whole host of mutual funds available, covering most risk profiles.

Value Line®

www.valueline.com

Value Line is a Web site for the investor with stock exchange information. The company has been managing mutual funds since 1950, and they have 12 mutual funds covering a range of risk profiles.

Vanguard

www.vanguard.com

After Fidelity, Vanguard is the second-largest mutual fund company, founded in 1975. Their funds are used in many companies' 401(k) plans. They have 150 domestic funds available as well as some international offerings, and they offer portfolio advice on their Web site.

The total assets invested in them is about $1 trillion. As a company, they are noted for being efficient, with some of the lowest expense ratios around. They even claim that the average expense ratio is 0.20 percent.

The oldest fund that Vanguard has, the Wellington fund, actually started as the Industrial and Power Securities Fund in 1929, which was unfortunate timing given the performance of the stock market in the following years. However, Vanguard considers themselves to have begun in 1975 when they formed with John C. Bogle as CEO. His policy to provide administration and distribution of the funds without adding a profit markup has been carried through to this day, which explains the low expense ratio. Though he has now retired, many are still fans of Bogle's philosophies, and there are several user groups dedicated to him on the Web.

Voyageur Asset Management Inc.

www.voyageur.net

Voyageur offer three types of families — equity and income funds called Tamarack, a retail money market, and institutional money market funds. They have seven equity funds covering all sizes.

Wasatch Funds

www.wasatchfunds.com

The Wasatch funds comprise 18 no-load funds, including income and growth.

Weitz Funds

www.weitzfunds.com

The Weitz family of funds has a choice of eight, including tax-free and government holdings.

Wells Fargo Advantage Funds

www.wellsfargoadvantagefunds.com

Wells Fargo is known for its banking products, but they also feature Wells Fargo Advantage Funds, a substantial family of funds including target-date among their offerings.

WesMark Funds

www.wesmarkfunds.com

With five funds, WesMark claims to be able to give you the core to your investment portfolio. They also have a money market mutual fund account.

Westcore

www.westcore.com

There are 12 mutual funds in the Westcore family of no-load funds, including bond and international funds.

Westport

www.westportfunds.com

Westport Funds are value-based and tend to be invested in the smaller companies.

Westwood Holding Group

www.whgfunds.com

Westwood has five funds, including small, medium, and large-cap, income, and balanced.

William Blair & Company

www.wmblair.com

William Blair has many financial products, including a selection of 13 mutual funds, as well as investment banking, brokerage, and asset management.

Wilshire Mutual Funds

www.wilfunds.com

Wilshire offers a number of funds, including large and small, value and growth, and a Dow Jones index fund.

Winslow Green

www.winslowgreen.com

Winslow was founded by an environmentalist and specializes in green investing, in which it is considered a pioneer. They have two mutual funds available.

Wright

www.wrightinvestors.com

Wright has an investors' service and offers five mutual funds for equity and income.

Yacktman

www.yacktman.com

Yacktman Funds have two different offerings, and most of their Web site information is in the form of downloadable documents.

CASE STUDY: SAM SUBRAMANIAN, PHD, MBA

Dr. Sam Subramanian publishes a newsletter with up-to-the-minute information on mutual funds and exchange-traded funds.

Subramanian is Managing Principal of AlphaProfit Investments, LLC. He edits and publishes the *AlphaProfit Sector Investors' Newsletter.* The newsletter uses sector

funds and sector ETFs to construct model portfolios for investors seeking aggressive growth and long-term capital appreciation. Subramanian's articles are published in leading financial Web sites, such as Forbes, MarketWatch®, The Motley Fool, and Yahoo! Finance®.

An avid mutual fund investor, Subramanian has analyzed mutual funds and exchange-traded funds for more than 20 years. After honing his skills in security research and analysis, Subramanian developed the ValuM Investment Process for managing investments. Prior to founding AlphaProfit Investments, Subramanian worked in positions of increasing responsibility in finance and corporate strategy advising in acquisitions and divestitures, asset valuation, trading, bankruptcies, and risk management.

He graduated with honors from the MBA program at the University of Michigan and has a Doctorate Degree in Chemical Engineering from Syracuse University. He also holds 17 U. S. and European patents.

Sam Subramanian PhD, MBA
AlphaProfit Investments, LLC
www.alphaprofit.com
subscriberservice@alphaprofit.com
281-565-6963

CASE STUDY: SAM SUBRAMANIAN, PHD, MBA

How did you get into the field of mutual fund investments?

Growing up in Mumbai, the financial capital of India, I got interested in stocks in my childhood. After migrating to the U.S., mutual funds were a logical choice for investing, since I had limited funds at my disposal. I liked sector funds for their reward potential and their ability to reduce portfolio risk. I developed the ValuM process to evaluate sectors and invested in sector funds to build my personal wealth.

Pleased with my success, I thought I should help others build their wealth as well. In 2003, I founded AlphaProfit Investments LLC, an investment research firm, to offer subscription-based mutual fund investment newsletters.

As a fund manager/investment adviser, what do you see as your primary function when selecting investments?

My primary functions include:
- Analyzing sectors and industries using the ValuM process
- Selecting sector funds and ETFs for playing the investment thesis
- Constructing actionable model portfolios

Given the current state of the financial markets, have you changed the way that you select any investments, or is your existing strategy already coping well?

I have not changed the sector evaluation and investment selection methodology.

Given heightened uncertainty since the latter part of 2008, I actively try to manage risk by appropriately diversifying the model portfolios across sectors and by including sectors with lower correlation to the broad market. In selecting individual sector funds or ETFs, I place added emphasis on their volatility or risk characteristics.

I also pro-actively educate subscribers to follow a disciplined strategy and prudently allocate assets to equities considering risk, investment objective, and time horizon.

What do you like and dislike about mutual funds?

Mutual funds allow folks with limited assets to diversify and engage a professional to select securities in hard-to-research areas like foreign stocks and high-yield bonds. They offer convenience features like automatic addition and withdrawals, making dollar-cost averaging easier.

CASE STUDY: SAM SUBRAMANIAN, PHD, MBA

And the wide availability of no-load, no-transaction-fee funds in brokerage accounts allows investors to change investments without incurring fees or commissions.

As for dislikes, mutual funds are usually not suited for short-term trading due to restrictions or redemption fees. Fund investors have limited control over realization of capital gains and can end up paying taxes even when their investment loses value. The timeliness of information on security holdings of actively managed funds is often less than desired. Some funds have egregious expense ratios, and a select few have allowed preferred customers to engage in "late trading."

What personal qualities do you think help you succeed as a fund manager/ investment adviser?

• Avoiding acting in panic
• Disciplining self to stick to investment strategies
• Taking prudent risks
• Being somewhat of a contrarian
• Conducting in-depth research to understand investments

What is the biggest success you have had concerning mutual funds?

With reference to the *AlphaProfit Sector Investors' Newsletter* ... winning *Hulbert Financial Digest's* No.1 rank on ten occasions among mutual fund newsletters and being named by MarketWatch as a top-ten investment newsletter.

For the 5-year period ending September 30, 2008, the *Newsletter's* Focus and Core model portfolio gained 78 percent and 48 percent, compared to the S&P 500's 29 percent advance.

What is the biggest challenge that you have had to face?

Navigating the market "mine field" where free market forces are being distorted by government intervention (e.g., restriction on short sales in financial shares) and sector leadership changes are frequent.

Convincing investors to (A) follow a disciplined strategy and stick to a plan, (B) stay level-headed through bull and bear markets, avoiding extreme optimism and extreme pessimism, and (C) avoid chasing "hot" sectors or funds and avoid panic action.

CASE STUDY: SAM SUBRAMANIAN, PHD, MBA

What advice would you give to potential investors, particularly in the face of the economic crisis, and how would this vary depending on their age?

I believe it is useful for most investors to review their investments and prudently determine their equity allocation. In addition to age, equity allocation normally depends on factors such as investment objective, risk tolerance, and financial situation. —Specifically,

- Most investors should keep in cash monies needed for the near-term, say the next two years

- Investors with shorter time horizons may err on the side of caution and use periods of strength to prune exposure to equities

- Investors saving monies for a longer-term need, say three years or longer, can invest part of them in equities

- Financially secure investors with a multi-decade investment time horizon or commitment to purchase equities on a regular basis can consider increasing their equity allocation to take advantage of attractive opportunities

Regardless of the situation, I urge investors to make changes to investments gradually and avoid acting in panic.

CHAPTER 10

How Can I Choose From So Many?

With such an expansive selection of mutual funds available from a vast range of companies, you may be bewildered by the choices you face. Perhaps that is why you chose to read this book. In this chapter, we cut through the clutter and focus on the factors you must consider in order to find the right fund or funds for you.

There is no such thing as an ideal fund. Any funds mentioned in this book are worth your consideration, but only you can decide whether they suit your circumstances. Before you baffle yourself with numbers, seriously consider what you are looking for in your investment. It is easy to say that you are looking for maximum returns on your money with no chance of losing capital, but that description must be qualified depending on your circumstances.

As we have seen toward the end of 2008, the financial markets can encounter problems that can spread to everyone involved.

There are few people who did not lose part of their investment in the stock market crash. It is fair to say that no funds were insulated from the effects, although some did fare better than others. Some funds are even set up to profit from a bear market, but you must anticipate this move in order to be correctly positioned. People would have been better off if they had selected funds that were regarded as less risky. However, in the normal-growth market that we have become used to, the less risky funds tend to produce lower returns.

This is a natural and underlying trade-off. If you take more risk with your investment, you would normally expect that, if successful, the reward would be greater. Your task is to select what appear to be the optimum funds for your circumstances, and note that just because you invest in risky funds, you are not guaranteed a greater return than a less risky investment would have. Similarly, a relatively safe fund may produce small returns, and another that is equally safe may give greater returns. Your analysis will allow you to determine the best returns for the risk you want to take.

Concentrate on What Matters

When you look at the number of mutual funds from which you can choose, you may be tempted to refer to a review site or *Forbes* magazine and accept their rankings. Though this will not likely lead to large errors because these are reputable companies, there is no universal best buy. With what you learn in this book, you can choose funds that are well-suited and tailored to your particular circumstances.

When others offer ratings of mutual funds, they look at the features, figures, and rates of each, assigning a point value or a multiplier. They combine these figures to give an overall number for the fund and compare these with other funds. The problem is that this number or rating does not take into account your needs and circumstances, and it is subjective to their assessment.

Be aware that simply finding the fund with the highest return in any one year is not a recipe for success. Funds that adopt a higher risk strategy stand a chance of performing better than otherwise good funds and, therefore, taking the top position for returns. The same high-risk strategy means that the returns can be inferior for other years.

There are methods to help you sort through your choices. First, the fund you have interest in should be a no-load fund. As stated previously, there is no statistical reason that you should pay a load — this does not equate to better performance. You can consider funds that have other penalties, perhaps for short-term redemptions, as this may discourage short-term traders from buying these funds and costing the company a disproportionate amount in administration charges.

Similarly, there is no reason to penalize yourself by choosing a fund with a high expense ratio. It is not necessary to choose the lowest expense ratio, but it is a factor that should be considered in your assessment of the fund. The expense ratio is affected by the total investment in the company's fund, as well as the type of fund. Remember that the expense ratio represents money coming out of your investment returns every year, so it is a significant aspect to consider.

There is no maximum percentage for the expense ratio that is reasonable. Percentages vary with the type of fund, like in an index fund, which is generally thought to require less work but results in a lower expense ratio.

For an actively managed fund, you may expect to pay up to 1 percent if it is one of the larger funds, and a little more if it does not have as much money invested. In a government bond fund, you would expect much less than in an active growth fund, in which the manager needed to spend considerable time researching the stocks.

Analyze funds that have existed for a reasonable amount of time to enable effective assessments of their track record. Look for at least five years to ten years as a minimum to ensure you can properly judge the fund's volatility — a reflection of the management's view toward risk. You should be able to see the returns for each year and evaluate how these compare with the market index to see whether the fund consistently beats the average. If the fund has been poorer than the average for three years in a row, it is probably not worth your investment.

Another practical factor is how large the initial investment needs to be. Given that you do not have unlimited funds — and if you heed the recommendations in this book, you may be purchasing positions in up to ten funds — you need to determine how much you must invest to start holding the fund. You will often find that once you are a fund holder, the additional amounts required for adding to the investment are much lower. Some funds can require as much as $1 million to become a shareholder, but this is not common. Many funds only require a few thousand dollars but, for instance, the Vanguard PRIMECAP fund has a minimum investment of $25,000, which would equate to you needing one quarter of a million dollars for ten funds. The normal recommendation is that you put an equal amount in each of the funds that you buy.

Your consideration of what you feel about various market sectors, together with your overall risk tolerance, will give you some guidance as to which types of funds you should invest in. You should avoid assuming the fund's description is completely correct, but rather should thoroughly examine the fund's details to see where your money will be invested. For instance, you may find an international fund still holds a large proportion of domestic securities, and this can be determined by looking at the prospectus or one of the comparative tables that you will find from various services like Morningstar on the Internet. Avoid the remorse of determining your investment needs, only to purchase inappropriate funds on the basis of their titles.

Remember that diversification is one of the sound principles of investing. If you do not diversify and you invest in a sector that goes up, you will be better off than the diversified investor. However, the question is whether you want to risk your savings on the basis of your anticipation of the market. If you are able to determine in advance which areas are going to prosper, you would likely be better off being a stock trader rather than an investor in mutual funds. For the rest of us who want reasonable security for our savings, a mix of sectors and sizes of companies means that the sector fluctuations are averaged out, and you will receive a more even return.

Some may raise another question: Mutual funds already provide diversity because they are invested in many different securities, so why seek further diversity by buying several mutual funds? The answer to this comes down to the individual nature of your needs. You can buy mutual funds that take a broader view of the financial market and seek to encapsulate it in one managed fund, but I do not recommend this. You would be buying a packaged solution, a one-size-fits-all fund that will only be the best for you if the investment manager's views coincide completely with yours. That is why I and many other fund pickers will tell you to buy a mix of funds that are in distinct, different sectors. In this way, you have control and can satisfy your own investment profile.

To best fit your personal needs, you will must go through this exercise in each of the sectors that you want to include in your portfolio. For instance, if you want a small-cap domestic stock fund, you must identify several candidates and compare returns, expense ratios, and other factors among them. This is a separate action from looking at large-cap funds, which should be compared only to each other. You will also want to keep separate the funds that you are selecting for growth, as compared to those you are selecting for value.

Another revealing exercise is to see how the fund performed in both bull markets and bear markets. It is certain that given a sufficient length of time, you will be holding your mutual fund portfolio through both of these aspects of the cyclical market, and you may not be able to anticipate the onset in time to switch your holding. Verify that the fund you choose performs as well as may be expected in a bear market, rather than rapidly losing all the gains of the previous years.

In all this assessment, the comparisons among similar funds is most important. Compare the returns of the funds for several years. Compare the fluctuations, which can be quantified by looking at the standard deviation; if the standard deviation is higher, then the risk is greater. Compare the risks, where one standard measure is called the "beta." A beta of one is the average for the stock market. If the beta is greater than one, then the risk is slightly higher than average; a low beta suggests a less risky prospect. You may expect to see betas from about 0.5 to 1.5, though values outside that range are technically possible.

Finally, you should not ignore the tax implications of the returns of the fund. These will vary with your personal circumstances and your current tax bracket — as well as the one you expect to be in for the future. The funds will have tax-adjusted returns as well as gross returns listed, and it is usual for the tax adjusted return to assume a maximum tax rate. If your situation is different, then you should make adjustments.

The Prospectus

The most important document that describes a mutual fund is the prospectus. Many elements in the prospectus are prescribed by law, and you will quickly learn how and where to compare funds. The prospectus gives you an initial basis from which you should decide which funds you want to look into further.

The prospectus may be split into two parts, which some mutual funds do for clarity. The first part is a streamlined version describing the fund, and the second, sometimes called the "statement of additional information," may only be offered to you on request, but it is required to be available.

Having said that, there are many other aspects of a mutual fund that may not be revealed in the way that you want in a prospectus — after all, it is also a selling tool for the mutual fund company — and I will later elaborate on how you can research these further. However, you will find that most prospectuses follow the same general arrangement, starting with the name of the fund, a table of contents, and a simple overview. Keep in mind that the prospectus is printed annually, so if it appears to be a few months old, that is not a problem. Visit the mutual fund company's Web site to obtain the latest information about a mutual fund.

The first important item you will find in the prospectus is the profile of the fund, which will list the objectives, strategies, and risks. The fact that the risks are listed should not scare you, as every fund has risks, and they are required to be spelled out. Familiarize yourself with the particular risks that the fund is taking. This may indicate an exposure to emerging markets or the credit quality of any bonds the fund invests in, for example. The fund will likely be at pains to ensure that all the risks are detailed to avoid complaints at a later date if the fund fails to perform as expected.

The objective of the fund is like a mission statement. It sets out what the managers see as the purpose of the fund — for example, whether it is focused on providing a regular income for share-holders or whether capital growth is counted as more important. However, and perhaps in common with many mission state-ments, the objective can read like a platitude and may not leave you feeling better informed.

The strategy section is more interesting, though it still maintains a generality in order to give the fund manager scope to invest in what he or she considers worthwhile at the time. In this section, you will gather a better idea of the type of fund the manager is running. For instance, in a fund that invests in stocks, you would expect to read whether the fund concentrates on large-cap or small-cap companies, together with any sectors on which it fo-cuses, such as technology. For a bond mutual fund, it might state that the fund invests in Treasury bonds.

Studying and comparing the strategies sections of different funds can be an interesting exercise, as it will identify the original pur-pose the fund was meant to serve. Regard this section as an aspi-ration, rather than as an accurate reflection of the current deploy-ment of funds. Many times, you will find that the strategy section covers a whole range of investments, some of which the manager has little intention of making. It will likely be set up to allow the manager freedom and will not necessarily be typical of how the fund is normally managed.

Next in the prospectus is information about the past performance of the fund. This may not reflect the latest performance, as the report is possibly several months old, but the latest figures are readily available online, and checking on those will be the next stage of your review. It can be quite useful to see how consistent the fund is over the years. A table or chart will give you the numbers for the past ten years, and you should not be surprised to see some years that have negative growth, as well as some high earning years. The consistency of the fund, together with the highest returns, will be affected by what type of fund it is, and the most variation should be in a mutual fund that invests in stocks and shares.

You may find that the managers have decided to include figures from a standard market index for comparison with their returns. The index will show how the market or sector as a whole has performed, and you should hope that the fund appears to perform better than average. Be assured that they have chosen the index that puts their fund in the most favorable light, and treat such comparisons with suitable caution. It can be helpful to have these comparisons, but make sure it is contrasted against an applicable index.

Regulations require that the mutual funds show their costs in a standard way to allow you to become familiar with the layout as you browse through several prospectuses. These include a chart of the costs for buying and selling shares, and one of the line items is a sales charge or load. If it is a no-load fund, then you will see "None" in this line. As I advised previously, I see little reason to pay a load, as you can often find a comparable no-load fund. If you have a financial advisor who suggests that you purchase this particular fund, check this to see whether they are pushing it forward because there is a commission attached.

The next section of costs includes the annual operating expenses, which every mutual fund charges on an ongoing basis. There is no escaping this, as you must have a manager and associated operation in order for it to exist. These expenses can vary from fund to fund, and this place in the prospectus is where you will determine any significant differences when comparing funds.

The prospectus will normally offer more details of the fund's operation, including on which dates it will pay any dividends each year, what the total capitalization is, how long it has been in existence, and even the ticker symbol you can use to buy the fund through a broker.

The rest of the prospectus includes more detail, some of which is simply historic, and other information that may help you in determining whether the fund will suit you. For instance, you may find a section that covers the investment strategies in more detail, setting forth the objectives that the managers have for the fund and how they intend to achieve them. You can use this information to be sure that the fund is not intending to invest your money in any way you would not be happy with — for instance, if you do not want exposure to the stock market, you can confirm that this is ruled out by reading this section. The prospectus will also include the background of the firm that is managing the investment, thus you will be aware of who is responsible for your money and can see how much experience they lay claim to.

You will also come across some detailed financial pages. First, you will see the summarized net asset value; the dividends paid, sometimes called distributions; and a calculation of the total return. Note that the total return does not include some of the charges you might have incurred, and you have to include in your personal calculations any sales or other fees. There are some details of value in this section — for instance, the Turnover Rate details how often the fund manager changes the investments each year. A turnover of 25 percent or less represents a steady buy-and-hold approach, whereas anything over a 100 percent turnover reveals heavy trading in search of larger profits but would involve incurring greater risk, along with potentially greater tax implications.

Annual Report

In addition to a prospectus, companies produce an annual report, which is similar to the annual report that you may be used to from regular stock investing. You may have received a copy with the prospectus, but often you must request the annual report separately. This includes a Chairman's letter, which explains how the fund has performed over the past year, usually expressed in glowing terms to encourage further investment. You may find comparisons to other funds or indexes to support the claims. Also expect a summary from the Fund Manager, which will explain the performance of the fund related to the market in a similar way to the Chairman's letter, but in more detail to anticipate market moves in the future.

Following this are more financial summaries. These detail the fund's particular holdings, and you will see from the extensive list the amount of diversification that you are achieving by investing in this fund. This summary also serves to give a further check of how the fund is keeping in line with its stated objective of investing in, say, large-cap companies, and whether it is slipping into some small-cap investment to try to boost the returns.

Online Services

With the advent of the Internet, you can investigate virtually anything from the comfort of your own home. Mutual funds, and other financial instruments, are easily researched on the Internet, but the number of results that you receive after a search — more than 12,000,000 for "mutual funds" on Google — can be confusing. However, the Internet can be harnessed to filter down your choices and help you decide which funds are worthy of further investigation. The following Web sites provide general and unbiased information, as it is important to ensure that any sites you refer to are unbiased — or that you at least understand any commercial interests.

Morningstar

Morningstar is a tremendous resource for researching mutual funds. They were founded on the idea that independent objective analysis should be available to all investors, and their Web site has details and tools that you would be well-advised to become familiar with, as they can speed up and enhance your search for suitable funds.

In addition, you can be sure that Morningstar is large enough and unbiased in its reports and recommendations. It is also useful for researching other investments, such as stocks, options, and hedge funds. The experts are committed to mutual funds as vehicles to achieve long-term financial goals, and you can obtain access to many of their features at no charge.

Aside from having their own lists of best-performing funds, they have an interactive fund screener for which you can set the criteria and view the results. When you start, you may find that you are setting the criteria so strictly that no funds will satisfy them, but it is easy to go back and change that what is less important to you until you find some funds to choose from.

When you have a list of funds that satisfy your initial criteria, you can then select "score," and Morningstar gives you the opportunity to rank the importance of different factors, such as the five-year returns, before giving you comparative scores for the funds you have selected.

A unique feature developed by Morningstar is its quick visual summary in the form of a style box, which is an easy-to-read chart. The box is a 3x3 grid, with the rows indicating the level of risk from load, from moderate to high, and the columns showing the type of investment. For stocks, the columns include value, blend, and growth; for bond funds, the traits are short, intermediate, and long-term.

The predominant type of investment is denoted by filling in one of nine boxes — for instance, a low-risk, short-term bond fund would have the top left corner filled in. The idea is to have a ready reference to the style of fund investment, enabling you to easily determine whether you are diversified with your holdings or too heavily weighted in any direction.

There is considerable information available at no charge on the Web site, including the major holdings of the fund, sector break-downs, and year-on-year returns, but you can also subscribe to obtain access to their analysts' views and recommendations, and they offer a 14-day trial period for you to see whether a subscription would be worthwhile.

American Association of Individual Investors

Another paid service is offered by the American Association of Individual Investors (AAII), whose Web site is at **www.aaii.com**. The AAII is a non-profit organization that provides investing advice of all kinds, including mutual funds, and they issue a mutual fund guide each year that lists thousands of funds. Though not as comprehensive as the Morningstar Web site, it is appreciably cheaper to subscribe to and can be recommended for doing your own research.

The AAII is also a good alternative resource for other types of investing, as it offers articles and discussions for the small investor. Because they are a non-commercial group, they are well-regarded for independent advice.

Other Online Resources

Apart from visiting a particular fund company's Web site, there are several other resources online where you can view basic information about the different funds. Using an independent site allows you to pull up comparisons among different mutual fund companies on the same page, rather than having to load each page separately from the companies' sites.

The fourth method of searching for a fund is by selecting a fund family, such as Vanguard. This would be useful to you if you decide to keep your money in the same family of funds to enable easy transfer among different types of accounts. The selection will show you all the funds that are available from the fund family, in this case, Vanguard.

CHAPTER 11

Assembling a Portfolio

Risk Tolerance and Effects

With a firm idea of how to assess and compare the performance of different mutual funds, you now must become specific on what you are trying to achieve and how you are prepared to get there. Most investments fluctuate, and when you invest in mutual funds, you must pre-determine what your personal risk tolerance is.

Measuring and assessing risk and benefits can be done in several ways, but what happens to your investment is not a statistical average; rather, it is an actual event. For instance, you could choose what is considered a safe investment, returning an average of 5 percent per year and only losing value once every ten years. If the first year you hold it and it loses value, you may be disappointed. You might even be unfortunate enough to suffer a second year of losses — such things can happen — and, again, you have to accept that the terms on which you entered the fund only expressed averages — with no guarantees.

On the other hand, if you are young, you may choose a risky investment that has down years as often as years when it makes money but, on average, achieves a 20-percent annual return. The first year or two that you hold this investment could give you far better than 20 percent on your money, and you would be elated. However, this does not mean that you have made any wiser a choice of fund than the previously mentioned investment, and you should expect in the course of time to have some down years as well. The categorization of risky and less risky is only a statistical reference and does not guarantee losses or gains in any particular time period.

If you are interested in receiving decent returns on your investment — ones that give you a clear profit over and above inflation — then you will eschew the guaranteed minimal returns of a savings account and will still consider mutual funds as one of your investment options. You must be prepared to take a longer-term view of your account and accept that the fluctuations are an intrinsic part of this type of investing.

Identifying Your Goals

Once you have come to terms with the idea of risk and have accepted that you are investing for the long-term, you need to determine what your goals are and how you can realistically achieve them. Form a plan that has a high probability of success; the longer your time horizon, the more you can rely on the actual performance of the funds you choose reflecting their statistical averages.

In other words, if you are at the start of your career and have no immediate need for money, preferring instead to invest steadily for your retirement, then you can take on a statistically risky investment that promises high average returns. This may vary wildly in value through the years, but provided the fund continues to reflect its previous performance, you will finish better off at retirement than if you had chosen a safe fund.

On the other hand, you may be at the start of your career, but also entertaining the thought that you might want to purchase a house in about five years. In this case, as you may need to access the money for a deposit on a property, your goal may be to have a safer place for your investment that is likely to have grown steadily through this short time, and you may need to look more toward bond-centered funds.

You should note that these ideas are not mutually exclusive. For instance, you should maintain a regular trickle of funds toward your retirement goals, but you may wish to put some money aside for shorter-term projects, such as a house or a once-in-a-lifetime vacation. This would imply that you can invest some money in both types of funds, identifying that you have more than one purpose for your savings.

It is not unusual to have several financial goals in different time frames. If you approach the construction of a portfolio without having this in mind, then you may find that you are just assembling an average portfolio, rather than one that is geared to your personal requirements.

One common mistake made by those who are nearing retirement is thinking that all their funds must be in a secure investment that does not give high returns but is not likely to fluctuate much in value. You must do the calculations for yourself, but if you have sufficient funds to live on, it is fine to have some investments in the riskier funds, such as stocks-based funds. After all, when you retire, you likely will not need access to all your money immediately. Assuming you have enough for decades of retirement, then you can identify money that you will not need to access for ten or more years. Placed in a riskier investment, this can, on average, generate higher returns and give you a better lifestyle later than if you kept all your money in safe investments. Note that the terms "risky" and "safe" in this context reflect how much the investments are expected to fluctuate over the years, and not whether you should invest in something where you could lose a substantial amount of money.

When you assess your goals, also take into account how much you think you need for each of them. You may be able to be specific on this. For example, by knowing about how much you will pay for a house in five years' time and desiring to save enough for a 20 percent deposit (to avoid paying private mortgage insurance), you can do the calculations and see how much you need to allocate each month into your safe portfolio element.

Other goals are not so easily defined. There are general guidelines developed by experts for how much you need in retirement, but the amount you spend depends on what type of lifestyle you are looking forward to. The much-quoted rule is that you need 70 to 80 percent of your working income to maintain your standard of living, but some retirees who decide to have an active lifestyle find they spend even more than what they used to earn.

Another rule of thumb is that in retirement, you can afford to spend 4 percent of your savings each year. The calculation of this includes allowing for increasing expenditure each year in line with inflation, and is worked out so that you are unlikely to run out of money within the most optimistic estimate of your lifetime.

But most Americans do not save sufficiently for their retirement. While many people's retirement accounts tend to get what is left over after all the bills are paid, if you clearly identify your goals and consider the returns that you reasonably expect from your fund choices, you will be well ahead of most when it comes to having the money necessary to live out your ideal retirement.

Asset Distribution

The next step in preparing your optimum portfolio of investment holdings is to consider the asset distribution that will work for you. I touched on this earlier when discussing the type of funds available, and it is an inherent part of your investing strategy.

Asset distribution arises directly from the consideration of your goals. It is not the selection of a market sector, as that is the next stage in preparing your portfolio; rather, asset distribution is concerned with your needs and your tolerance for risk. If all your savings are to be in mutual funds, you must consider how much of your assets should be in a form that is easily made into emergency cash.

In the current economic climate, there are few who can take continued employment for granted, and this has concentrated people's attention onto their emergency cash reserves. The truth is that most people could be laid off at any time in any employment market, even if you are good at your job and are making the company money. However, when one reads of companies making massive layoffs, the possibility of it happening to you increases in your consciousness, and you likely pay more attention to your emergency plans.

Many people are said to be one or two paychecks away from financial problems, as the nation as a whole seems to have forgotten how to save. Because you are reading this book, it is obviously your intent to save, and part of your savings should go toward establishing a reasonable emergency reserve. Advice varies, but it is a good guideline to have the equivalent of six months' salary put aside in an accessible account, which, for mutual funds, would be called a money market account.

Asset distribution also considers how much you have directed toward growth funds, which tend to include the relatively riskier stock investments. If you are young, then your portfolio may be heavily weighted toward this type of mutual fund. While the inherent riskiness means that there can be large fluctuations in this element of your portfolio, statistically investing in this way should produce higher returns in the long run, thus this is a reasonable course of action when you have time before you need to access the money.

Finally, you need to consider the percentage of income-producing funds that you want to comprise your portfolio. Nearing retirement, income becomes increasingly important, and you will find that you are turning more toward this type of investment. Such investing tends to be regarded as a capital preservation strategy, which protects your equity while providing income to live on.

Kinds of Portfolios

If mutual funds provide a built-in diversity, you may be wondering why you need to consider compiling a portfolio rather than investing in just one diversified fund. It is true that you can obtain the many combinations of investment with a mutual fund, including even a fund of funds, but with your knowledge of the workings of the fund industry, you will want to be able to more clearly define how your money is distributed. There is no one-size-fits-all solution to everybody's investing needs, and owning several mutual funds allows you to get the right mix of risk and return for your situation.

While most advisors agree that investing in more than one fund is a wise decision, there is some discussion about how many funds represent an optimal distribution. Morningstar addressed the question by constructing portfolios with up to 30 different funds to see what the effect would be. They considered the standard deviation of the portfolios, a measure of how much variation you can expect from year to year in the gains and losses.

They found that having at least four funds in the portfolio gave a good result, with the resulting volatility at an acceptable level. Additional funds contributed to the portfolio had little effect, and any more than seven funds produced no noticeable improvement. However, they cautioned that of more significance is where the funds are invested, as you may have a dozen funds that, if they are similarly invested in the growth sector at the present time, could all be caught out by a dramatic move in that sector. Thus, you would not have the diversity that you thought you did.

The AAII issues a guide to the top mutual funds every year in which they also consider the optimal number of funds. Though they say that no particular number applies for everyone, they derive their recommendation from considering the different types of funds available and ensuring that all types are represented in a portfolio.

For this purpose, the AAII consider that a diversified portfolio would include funds for domestic small-cap stocks, mid-cap stocks, and large cap stocks; international stocks in developing countries and in developed nations; and a domestic bond fund. These six types of funds could be increased if you were to separate the international funds into Europe and the Far East. You might also consider a money market fund and a tax-exempt bond fund. However, they do not advise more than ten funds and warn that over-diversification will likely lead to duplication in the investments, which adds nothing to overall performance and creates complication in tracking your holdings.

Short-Term Portfolio

The short-term portfolio is perhaps the most challenging one to select with any confidence because any unfortunate choice, such as a higher-risk stock fund, would not have time to recover to meet the goals should it go through a period of fluctuation. The alternative of ultra-safe places like a bank CD may not give a return that even keeps up with the rate of inflation. There are some conservative funds that you should consider when putting together a short-term portfolio.

For the purposes of discussion, I have taken "short-term portfolio" to mean that you foresee wanting to access your money within the next five years. This may be because you want the money as a large deposit or that you are looking ahead to a major expenditure, such as buying a new car or building an addition on your house.

In this short term, you cannot afford to make mistakes that require a longer time to recover. If your investments fluctuate, you may find that the value is down when you need to draw on the money. For this reason, if you own any stock funds at all in this portfolio, they should be small and based on sound, solid companies, such as you will find in large-cap stock funds.

To achieve a reasonable rate of return without exposing yourself to the risks of the stock market, you will need to focus on money market funds and on bond funds. With these as the core of your portfolio, you should have dealt with the most important consideration for this portfolio: preserving your capital.

When selecting a bond fund, you must consider the term of the underlying bonds. As explained in a previous chapter, when interest rates rise in the market, the price of bonds tends to fall or be discounted in financial parlance. Bonds are less affected in their value if they have only a short time before they mature because, at maturity, the full value becomes due. The longer out the maturity date, the more the price of the bond will fluctuate with the prevailing interest rate.

To preserve capital in your short-term portfolio, focus on finding short-term and intermediate-term bond funds. You should take care to examine the prospectus because these terms are vague and subject to interpretation; what is labeled a short-term bond with one company may be the equivalent of an intermediate-term bond at another. Bond funds can also vary in their content so that some have a wide range of maturity dates, and some are focused on a small range of similar dates.

As a rule, you may expect that a short-term bond fund has an average maturity date of up to three years in its holdings. An intermediate-term bond fund will have an average maturity date from three to ten years, with long-term being longer than ten years. A longer term tends to mean greater yield because of the greater risk.

When looking for a low-cost bond fund, consider actively managed intermediate-term bond funds, and also look at purchasing an index bond fund. If you might need to access some of your money sooner, consider extremely short-term bonds, which will hardly fluctuate with interest rate changes. The core of the fund should be based around good quality companies, as some funds use lesser-rated companies in order to get higher yields. If there is a problem in the market, then the lesser-rated companies will be more likely to reflect that in their returns.

Intermediate-Term Portfolio

As I have included up to five years in the short-term portfolio, I will define the intermediate-term portfolio as being from five to ten years. There is more flexibility in how you invest, at least in the early years, when considering this length of time. This might be a portfolio that you establish to pay for college fees for your children.

With this length of time, you still do not want to take any undue risks that could affect the fund's value when you need the money, but you are able to achieve higher returns by including some slightly riskier and better-rewarding funds. Again, you will be diversifying your investment among funds to ensure that you are not exposing yourself to the possibility of failure.

In this case, I would suggest putting one-quarter to one-third of your investment into a money market or bond fund to provide sound preservation of your capital. These can be selected in a similar way to the short-term portfolio funds. To achieve a greater rate of return, the remainder of your money may be placed in one of the more secure stock-based mutual funds, such as one that invests in large-cap companies. This should be the core of your intermediate-term portfolio to allow you the opportunity to achieve better returns and growth than with the conservative short-term portfolio.

You could provide further diversification for your portfolio by looking at small-cap companies and/or foreign stock funds, and this would also give you the possibility of better returns.

Remember that when you are approaching the target year for this portfolio, you must change the percentage of your holdings. You do not want to be holding stock funds in such a large proportion within a year or two of your goal in case the market has a cyclical swing. Provided you have had reasonable gains from your stock funds, you might consider changing these over to more conservative holdings in line with the short-term portfolio when you are a few years away. If the market is in a depressed part of the cycle, you will have sufficient time to wait a couple of years for it to recover before you put your money in a less risky fund leading up to your target date.

Long-Term Portfolios

With the long-term portfolio, in which you do not need to access your money for more than ten years, you can afford to take more risks with the types of funds that you invest in. This does not mean that you will be putting your money into funds that may consistently lose but, rather, you will be investing in funds that have large swings in value but average out to greater returns over time.

This type of portfolio may be for your retirement, so you should carefully consider the tax situation, which can be a major factor in what and how you invest. If you are buying these funds through a retirement account, you may have built-in tax advantages. If the funds will be held in a regular manner, you may want to investigate funds that have a tax benefit, such as those that invest in government bonds.

To get the higher returns that you want on a long-term portfolio, you should probably be putting 75 to 80 percent of your money into stock funds. Over the long-term, these should average out to higher returns than bond funds have. You may also consider the types of stock funds that may have higher returns associated with greater fluctuations in price. These might include some small-cap funds and other riskier investments.

Assuming you have a target date in mind, you can adopt a similar procedure to that mentioned under the intermediate-term portfolio. Keep in mind that when you are within ten years of your target date, you want to reduce the risk in line with the intermediate-term portfolio, and you need to adjust your holdings accordingly. As the date nears, you should adjust again to the least risky short-term portfolio plan. If the market is in a slump, you will have no particular need to convert your holdings on a certain date. That is the point of the flexibility built into the system. You should give due consideration to adjusting the proportion of the holdings when you perform your regular review.

Timing Your Investments

If you are having trouble putting together a portfolio that will sufficiently meet your goals with the expected rate of return, you may be tempted by the idea that you can time your investments into the funds that are doing well in any particular year.

Market timing is an idea that has been around for as long as people have invested. Its origin is in the 20/20 hindsight with which the markets have been viewed following any year when a particular market sector stood out as the best. It is easy in retrospect to construct a method of investing and re-investing your money to take advantage of particular market moves. For instance, the price of oil seems to take off occasionally, and if you could anticipate it and change your investments appropriately, your earnings would be much higher.

Unfortunately, in the many studies that have been conducted of market timing, the conclusion is that this strategy is almost impossible to do. To the extent that you can identify and anticipate daily or weekly fluctuations in the individual share prices, it is possible to make money from trading stocks and shares. But the ability to anticipate longer trends before they arise has been found to not be viable in any practical sense.

Many studies have focused on whether you should stay continuously in the market, even when the returns are somewhat unexciting. The popular theory is that if you could anticipate a market downturn, you could move your funds into a money market or cash account, then buy stocks again before the upturn. The following statistics show how dangerous such a plan can be to your wish for consistent growth.

If you had invested $100 in the stock market in 1963, 30 years later, it would be worth $2,430. This is assuming that your investment was spread evenly across the whole market. If you had taken your money out of the market for just ten days, and these were the best days of the period, the value in 1993 would only have been $1,540. If you missed out on the top 40 days and had your money out of the market, you returns would have been only $650.

That study picked the best-performing days of the market, so it represents the absolute worst case that you could have, in hindsight, experienced. Another study in 2001, published in the *Financial Analysts' Journal*, considered instead every possible combination of being in and out of the stock market, month by month, assuming that when money was not invested in stocks, it would be securely lodged in treasury bills. The authors considered how this compared to a buy-and-hold strategy and took into account all the years from 1926 to 1999.

The findings were still significant. Of all the combinations of being in and out of the market, only one-third of them turned out better than a simple buy-and-hold strategy. Thus, the odds are against your ability to improve your returns by switching in and out of market exposure. If you were to switch each year rather than each month, the odds would be worse still. Of all the possible combinations, only one in five beat the simple buy-and-hold plan.

CASE STUDY: MICHAEL KOTHAKOTA

Michael Kothakota is an investment adviser, focusing mainly on military clientele.

I am the Chief Investment Officer of WolfBridge Financial, a Registered Investment Advisor. We focus mainly on military clients, military retirees, and veterans. Our services and our portfolios are optimized to benefit military personnel and their families. My approach to investment management is to ensure that all client portfolios are customized to the benefit of that individual client. By crafting an investment plan to support retirement plans, education plans, and other life plans, I match the solution with the need so that clients have the opportunity to reach their goals.

Michael Kothakota
Chief Investment Officer
WolfBridge Financial
919-267-6740
michael.kothakota@wolfbridgefinancial.com
www.WolfBridgeFinancial.com

How did you get into the field of mutual fund investments?

I started my investment career at Edward Jones Investments, a company that believes in holding mutual funds for the long-term. That began in 2005.

As a fund manager/investment adviser, what do you see as your primary function when selecting investments?

As an investment advisor, I see the primary function of my job as the selection of investments that meet the client's needs, goals, and desires. Utilizing comprehensive information-gathering techniques, I construct portfolios that take these things into consideration.

CASE STUDY: MICHAEL KOTHAKOTA

Given the current state of the financial markets, have you changed the way that you select any investments, or is your existing strategy already coping well?

Yes, I have. My old way was to find mutual funds that had a history of good performance and long-term stability, and I have decided to move to a more strategic and tactical perspective. Mutual funds are just not cutting it.

What do you like and dislike about mutual funds?

About the only thing I like about mutual funds is the fact that you can get a good amount of diversification for a good price. As for dislikes, take your pick: Exorbitant management fees that add little to no value; 12b-1 fees; over-diversification; strict guidelines that trap skilled managers; inefficient from a tax perspective.

What personal qualities do you think help you succeed as a fund manager/ investment adviser?

I am open-minded, and I tend to think of solutions that are not always apparent to the average investment advisor. I have a great ability to work with people and can understand and empathize with what they are going through. At the same time, I can separate my emotions from the portfolios I manage, enabling me to make decisions that benefit my clients.

What is the biggest success you have had concerning mutual funds?

A gold fund I used for a client when gold was trading low. We bought the fund, and when the fund was up 30 percent, we sold it. While I do not recommend that strategy for everyone, there are times when getting into something quickly and exiting are good ideas.

What is the biggest challenge that you have had to face?

The biggest challenge I have had to face is trust in the investment world. With the scandals and the bank failures, it is hard for investors to trust advisors — especially independent advisors. I have had to differentiate myself as a true, trustworthy advisor who puts my clients' needs ahead of my own.

CASE STUDY: MICHAEL KOTHAKOTA

I have to emphasize that I have no loyalty to any one company, and that my loyalty is to my clients alone.

What advice would you give to potential investors, particularly in the face of the economic crisis, and how would this vary depending on their age?

Younger investors — I would say to save aggressively. Do not wait to start. I would also tell them to start with one stock, whether it performs well or not. Then buy another. And another. And another. Build it slow, but build it well. Consult an investment advisor along the way. Middle-aged, it is time to restructure your portfolios and also to throw out the mindset that you will retire completely on the assets you accumulate and invest. You need to look at retirement and investing as two separate things. Your investment plan can help support your retirement plan, but do not think that it cannot or will not run out. By utilizing an advisor who helps you define and reach your goals, you can optimize a portfolio that works for you through all markets. As for older investors, most older investors have been through difficult markets and good markets. They know a lot more than people who are just starting out investing or have been around a while. Older investors have to understand that their investments need to be structured to meet their needs and cannot be used to make a "quick buck" in the market. Also, this advice is dependent upon how savvy and/or how wealthy these investors are.

CHAPTER 12

Sample Portfolio Selection

This chapter will take you through the steps of selecting your portfolio, including what references you should use and how to find the specific information you need. I will assume that you want a middle-of-the-road medium return and medium risk portfolio, and that while you are not in the first flush of youth, you are not expecting to retire in the next few years.

If this is not your situation, the comments in the previous chapters covered how you should adjust your risk factors and your portfolio for your circumstances. For instance, you may not be saving for retirement, but may be saving to purchase a house in five years. For simplicity, I have referred to the time when you start taking funds as retirement in discussions below, but in reality, it maybe a different stage of your life for which you are saving.

Overall Plan

First, decide what kind of result you want from your planning. In this case, for an average sort of risk, you decide to accept the general recommendation for a diversified portfolio and want exposure to all three sizes of domestic stocks. You are concerned that the United States may fall behind in value compared to the emerging markets and want a reasonable exposure to equities from other countries, particularly the developing countries.

With the longer time horizon that you have, you are not interested in pure money market accounts, but you will have a proportion of your investment in bond funds and would prefer that these have some tax advantage.

At this stage of planning, experts advocate determining your future needs from your retirement goals and working out backward how much you must save each year and what type of risk you should take on in order to get to the desired goal. These factors are all interlinked, and if you do not take them step-by-step, you may become overwhelmed.

Before you proceed, understand that there is no one correct answer and that just because you pick one way of possibly achieving the required result does not mean that other ways are not equally valid. The future is hard to predict, and while history shows us the average returns that various investments can make, the results you experience may be quite different.

Part of your regular review of your portfolio should be to consider your long-term goals and whether your initial strategy is likely to succeed in attaining them. To get the best out of your investment, do not consider your work done after the initial selection. You will not just be looking at the actual performance of the funds you select; you will also be considering whether your initial targets need revision, and whether your needs have changed.

What Do You Need and When?

An interesting study released in April 2009 commented on the public's confidence in their retirement plans, showing that workers are less certain that they will save enough money to retire comfortably than they used to be. Only 13 percent of U.S. workers feel "very confident" that they will have enough money to enjoy a comfortable retirement.

This is despite the fact that workers are saving more than they used to, and that most people expect they will work longer to improve their chances of a retirement that will not have financial issues. Many people are still not clear on how to plan for retirement, and when they do, they often make incorrect assumptions about their retirement income.

Underlying this uncertainty are concerns about the poor economy being faced in 2008/2009. The confidence level is the lowest since the survey began 20 years ago. Distressingly, of those who are already retired, only 20 percent feel highly confident that they will remain financially secure.

About half of all workers admit that their savings and investments amount to less than $25,000, when you exclude the value of their home, and as many as one in five say that they have less than $1,000 put aside in savings. Considering that you are thinking of investing in mutual funds, I would venture to suggest that you are not in this group, but the vast majority of people are more or less aware that they do not face a prosperous retirement.

Less than half of the people surveyed said they have tried to calculate how much money they must save for their retirement. This is an important exercise so that you can be clear on how much you should be saving while you are working, and can also take a view on how aggressive your portfolio should be to have a chance of generating sufficient returns.

To determine how much money you need, you should do some serious consideration about your expected lifestyle and ambitions after you cease to work. Once you have a definition of your expectations, you can find online various calculators that will simply compound together expected inflation, expected returns from your investment, and even expected lifetime and help you determine what you need to live on for a given retirement fund amount. You can find these calculators on CNN Money®, MSN® Money, and on fund and financial planning Web sites.

Also take into account whether your house will be paid off by the time of your retirement, as mortgage payments are likely a significant fraction of your monthly expenditure. Your plans for retirement — whether they include cheap activities such as hiking or more expensive pursuits like golf or travel — have a large influence on the amount of money that you will need, and only you can estimate the extent to which you intend to practice these hobbies.

A significant part of your calculation is the allowance for expected inflation. As this is compounded each year in a similar way to compound interest, it can have a dramatic effect on the value of your funds. A salary of $50,000 per year now may need to be $200,000 per year in 20 years' time to account for inflation, to allow you to buy the equivalent goods with your income.

The farther away you are from your expected retirement, the more difficult it is to figure in the effects of inflation. Obviously, even if you calculated a saving rate that pays you your full salary of $50,000 per year at retirement in 20 years, it is unlikely that amount would be sufficient for your regular life style. In a similar way to trading in the stock market, many people have opinions, but no one knows the truth, and you should be careful about who you listen to when seeking advice about the declining value of money.

You may choose to look at historic inflation values and assume that these are going to carry through until your retirement. An excellent resource for these numbers is the Web site www.inflationdata.com. It is an interesting exercise to go back further than the last ten years and see how much inflation can be — for instance, in 1974 and 1980. This serves to emphasize the uncertainty that should be applied to your calculations.

While these numbers will give you an overall guide to perceived inflation, even with cautions about previous history being no real indication of the future, there are several factors to remember when trying to estimate your retirement needs. First of all, these published figures have varied in their methods of measurement over the years. Particularly in the last few decades, there has been much discussion and manipulation, generally serving to reduce the numbers, perhaps because they are used for index linking benefits.

Second, the inflation figures are calculated for a mix of spending that is deemed typical for an average household. In retirement, your spending may be atypical; for example, your mortgage may be smaller or nonexistent. Your financial needs may be greater or less than an amount adjusted for a typical household. If you care to go into that much detail, try breaking out the different categories of spending and choosing individual inflation rates for each of them.

However, given the uncertainty that exists in any case regarding inflation, you may find it a laborious exercise that in the end makes little difference to your decision. If you are risk averse, you will likely add a significant margin to what you anticipate the inflation rate will be in order to come up with a number.

Current circumstances may not help your view of future inflation. The response to the economic crisis has been swift and includes finding considerable money that did not exist before. Coupled with the tremendous cost of the Iraq war for the last few years, a good deal of additional money has entered the system that has no backing or foundation, other than confidence in the U.S. government to be able to pay it.

While commentators vary in their views of how large an effect this will have on the economy in the future, there is a consensus that paying trillions of dollars for various economic measures will cause inflation to rise, perhaps dramatically. Therefore, when making your calculations for the future value that you require to retire on, I would advise a conservative approach that allows for a significant increase in the inflation rate in the next few years.

Should you want a fast way to determine what your retirement income needs to be for your preliminary calculations, seek advice from various sources. One often-quoted guideline is that you need 70 to 85 percent of your pre-retirement income. But I would advise against using such a general guideline, as everyone's vision of their retirement can be different.

If you work it out, you may be pleasantly surprised. You might find that you can expect to live in the same manner with only 50 percent of your salary, updated in line with inflation. After all, your core spending is simply what you need for yourself and your spouse, and with a simple accounting program, you should be able to separate this out and determine it quite accurately. In retirement, you will probably not be supporting your children or your parents, which you may do now simply because you have the source of income. Your commuting costs to work, buying coffee, and other incidentals will disappear, and you may even wish to hang on to your car for longer, as you will likely be doing significantly less mileage.

Finally, remember that you do not have to find all of this income from your retirement account and savings. While it is true that most employers have moved away from providing "defined benefit retirement plans" in favor of "defined contribution retirement plans," such as 401(k)s — which leaves you with choices of how best to invest for maximum growth — the much-criticized Social Security method is still in existence and can be expected to provide a contribution to your income.

The survey referenced before found that a majority of retirees relied on Social Security for at least half of their income. The benefits paid may decrease in the future, as the reality of people living longer in retirement is changing the ratio between those contributing to Social Security and those benefiting from it, but it should continue to provide a useful supplement to other sources of income in retirement.

If you are paying Social Security taxes, you should receive a statement each year that gives you an estimate of the benefits that will be available to you for retirement at various ages. These are based on your taxable earnings for the previous year, and they assume that your earnings continue until retirement. If you need more information, visit the Web site **www.socialsecurity.gov**, where they have retirement calculators, free publications, and assistance.

What Do You Expect to Contribute?

The average worker with an employer-sponsored retirement plan is saving about 7 percent, which researchers say is about half of what they need to save in order to enjoy a retirement with a sustained lifestyle. The choice is between spending your money now and being somewhat constrained in retirement, or saving avidly with a frugal life style so that you can be assured of a comfortable old age.

Despite the current concern over viability of the Social Security system, most people rely on it for more than half their retirement income. You will want to ensure that your savings and investments can cover your needs if you do not wish to depend on a system that many believe should be considered bankrupt.

Even if you find that you are not using most of your salary for your living expenses, the IRS places limits on the amount that you can save each year in a retirement account. If you are 50 or older, the IRS allows increased contributions, which they call "catch-up contributions," so that you can bolster your account as retirement approaches.

For deferred contribution plans, such as a 401(k), you can save as much as $16,500 in 2009, increasing to $22,000 when you reach 50. IRA plans are limited to $5,000, or $6,000 for those 50 or older, which are the same limits applied in 2008.

Conventional wisdom states that if your employer gives a match or partial match to your retirement savings to their plan, you should contribute at least as much as needed to get the maximum contribution from your employer. This is certainly good advice, as it represents an instant return on your savings, even though you will not access it until your retirement.

Many people stop there and consider that contributing for the maximum employer match is the level of saving that they need to do. If you approach the retirement question from this point of view, then you may have a comfortable retirement but may not be able to accomplish some greater ambitions.

Nonetheless, as a good starting point, you can take the contributions that you think you can reasonably afford and work through the calculations to see how close the expected returns are to what you anticipate needing in the future.

What Returns Do You Think Are Realistic?

If you were to select funds randomly from each category that you wish to hold in your portfolio, you would be quite disappointed with the returns. Over the past five years, for 17 styles of stock funds, including different sizes of companies and different sectors, only two actually gave a positive return. That is, if you had put your money under the mattress five years ago instead of buying an average fund, the chances are that you would have more money today.

I believe that it is partly because of such performance figures that you now feel driven to research how to best select mutual funds for the future. However, different styles of funds will have different returns for varying market criteria; for instance, in some markets, large-cap will perform better than small-cap. Thus, despite the diversity that a mutual fund can have in its holdings, you want to diversify between mutual funds, including some foreign, large, and small companies.

It is certain that you do not get the best returns by doing this. At any particular time, one sector will perform better than another, so if you could always be invested in the best sector, you would gain more. Given that the future is unknown, this is not realistic; therefore, a diversity of funds represents the more practical solution.

One of the research tools that I recommend is **www.morningstar. com**. You should not limit yourself to just one Web site, however, particularly when it comes to looking for recommended funds. There are several other major Web sites that you can crosscheck the information with.

If you click on the Funds tab on the main screen, you can access the details of all mutual funds that Morningstar tracks. You can also access analysts' opinions of the best funds to own, but these require a paid subscription. There is a free trial available, but even without taking this, you can find the percentage returns for mutual funds over many periods, which will give you a starting point for researching the best-performing funds for you.

I would advise you to go on to the Morningstar Web site and experiment with the tools available. It is easy to click through categories for further information on individual funds, and you can see expense ratios, sector breakdowns, the returns on each of the last five years, and other statistics.

Be warned that you should not go by the best figures represented for the returns of the top funds. The funds that make the tops of lists are not typical of the class; otherwise, they would not make the top. The best and worst performance tends to be associated with a fund that has taken more risk than the rest of that class of funds.

If you select the funds at the top of each list, you are intrinsically not diversifying and betting that whatever caused the fund to get to that position will continue. While you do not need to take the average return for any class of fund, as you will be applying your knowledge to select a fund that performs better in its class, to rely on the best performance when you are planning for your retirement would be a mistake. Look at the typical returns for the top 20 funds in the class over a period and put a reasonable number into your calculations. Do not worry about decimal points; an approximation to the nearest percent is more accurate than you should expect.

Based on historical information, you might be tempted to assume that stock-based portfolios will increase by about 10 percent per year, which is optimistic given the current economic climate. A more realistic number is probably about 8 percent. Bond yields are much lower, particularly at the time of this writing, when the Treasury bond yields are close to zero. It is reasonable to assume a yield of about 4 percent in the future. Inflation may account for about 3 to 4 percent per year.

How Can You Make Up The Shortfall?

At this point, you have an assessment of your financial needs in retirement, an idea of what you can afford to invest on a regular basis, and an assumption of the returns that your investment will make up until your retirement. These are all guesses, unknown and unknowable, but they represent reasonable assumptions made to the best of your ability.

Plugging these numbers into one of the online calculators I spoke of before — or better still, if you are competent in using a spread-sheet, setting up a calculation sheet so that you can marry the figures together and experiment with changes — you will likely find that there is a shortfall between what you think you need and what you can expect from your investment.

I prefer to use a spreadsheet because you can introduce differ-ent factors that may not be accounted for in the preset programs available on the Internet. For instance, it is easy to put in the latest estimate of your Social Security and experiment with taking the payments at different retirement dates.

You may be familiar with the fact that the Social Security payment increases significantly if you wait until you are 70 before taking it. One option is to draw more funds out of your savings in the intervening years so you can enjoy the greater amount later, and a spreadsheet allows you to easily make an assessment of this. If you use a line for each year, you can generate a formula to update the capital, earnings, and withdrawals required; copy the formula down the page for each successive year; and even see when you will run out of money, according to this model.

Many people will find that they face significant challenges once they have gotten this far in the calculation. But it is better to know that there are going to be challenges now, rather than waiting until retirement and realizing them when it is nearly too late.

But you can try to balance the prediction by adjusting any of the variables. For example, you may wish to consider the amount of money you believe you might need in retirement. Perhaps you will settle for two vacations a year instead of three, or plan road trips rather than flying abroad.

If your housing expenses seem to be the item putting you over the top, you might want to consider moving to a smaller property as you approach retirement. This could be beneficial by releasing more capital, which could then be invested, and also potentially result in lower utility and other costs. The key to considering how you can try to balance your funds is to brainstorm ideas rather than trying to tweak your existing preconceptions.

Also, determine whether the amount you are planning to save each month is all that you can afford. Consider how important your retirement is to you compared with, for instance, the morning coffee bought on the way to work and the lunch eaten out with colleagues. It is easy to take a coffee from home and to prepare a packed lunch each day, and the savings can add up.

If the shortfall is significant, you may even want to consider a second part-time job so that you can dedicate the resulting funds from your investment plan. The key to making your retirement work is having time to adjust your attitudes, habits, and practices if you have done your planning in advance. You will not be caught out, as so many have been and will be, when it is too late to make a significant difference.

A variable you may able to influence is the amount of return that you expect from your investments, but it can be a gamble. If we assume that the return from a secure investment, such as a CD or a savings account, would be inadequate for your future plans, then you are left with the need to balance risk against possible gain.

Risk is only an assessment of the danger of not getting returns and cannot guarantee that you will actually achieve what you want. If you are begin planning early enough, your account will have a chance to recover, should the downside risk occur in the initial years of your investing.

If your plans show that there will be a shortfall, or if the risks that you take do not pay off, then you must continue working for a longer period. This has the double benefit that you will be paying into the retirement plan for longer, and your money will be in the plan longer, compounding its value.

No one can tell you with certainty whether your account is going to lose value next year, but the higher the risk, the greater the chance that it will. But with greater risk comes an increase in your potential reward. As long as you have done your homework on whatever you are investing in, then you have taken as much care as you can to get the odds on your side.

The purpose of all this preparation is to allow you to achieve the returns you want without taking undue risk. The process of thinking through how much you may need, how much you can afford to invest, and what returns are required of your investment is an important one — one that many people do not do. Normally, people pay as much as they think they can afford and are left with a problem when it is too late to make any difference.

From the earlier chapter discussing what mutual funds can invest in, you should have a clear idea of where your needs lie. As a reminder, stocks offer the prospect of greater returns in the fullness of time than do bonds or money market accounts, but they do carry a greater risk. If you have less than ten years before you need to access the account, then concentrating on stocks can be a large risk. If you have more than ten years to go, you are still in what is called an "accumulating stage," and most advisors say that you can consider up to 80 percent in stock-based funds to try to benefit from the additional growth.

You need a mindset that accepts that during some years, the rate of growth will not be desirable, but that does not necessarily mean that you have made the wrong choice. As long as the fund you choose is performing well within its class then, statistically, things should average out, and you will have some years during which the performance will improve.

For the purposes of this sample selection, I am going to refer to a standard medium-risk selection projects to provide sufficient returns for our purposes.

Selecting Your Base Portfolio

When selecting funds to use in your portfolio, I suggest you start with the less risky foundational funds before you move to the higher-risk — and potentially high-return — element. The foundational funds should give you a solid base return on a yearly basis, but they will not normally give you much in the way of excitement, either up or down. Rather, you can feel confident that you have a core value available in your savings.

The funds you will be looking for as a sound basis for your portfolio will include stock funds, but you should avoid the smaller companies. You will look for a good large-cap fund that may combine value and growth attributes, and you can also consider exposure to the stock market by investing in a market index fund designed to echo the returns of the market as a whole.

In common with many mutual funds, large-cap stock funds lost about 40 percent in 2008. Prior to that, they had been showing steady growth, averaging about 10 percent for the previous years. They are generally regarded as having average risk — after all, they are stock funds and not bond funds — but they do benefit from the better returns typical of the stock market.

For the year 2008, the best performing large-cap stock fund was the American Century® Equity Income (symbol TWEIX), which only lost 20 percent and is regarded as a low-risk fund. The top eight funds all managed to stay below a loss of 30 percent, significantly outperforming the average for this class of fund.

To select the actual fund you want to use, either access the information online or request a prospectus for each of the better-performing funds you are interested in. This will allow you to study the management objectives and will also show you the stocks that the fund holds. Pay particular attention to how often the stocks are turned over, as this will make a difference in your tax treatment. With large-cap stocks, the turnover is usually not as much as with the smaller companies.

The second part of your base holding for your portfolio should include bonds. Look for funds that invest in high-quality bonds with a reasonable period until maturity. As a guide, about six years to maturity date will give you nearly as high a return and less fluctuation than bonds with longer dates, so this is the period you should look at. As you are looking at holding the portfolio for the longer term, you should not be worried about some fluctuation in the value of the bonds. If this was an issue, for example, in a shorter-term portfolio, you would look at funds that were maturing soon so that they would not be so varied in value when the interest rates changed.

If you want to avoid paying too much tax, particularly if you are in a higher tax bracket, concentrate on municipal bond funds that can give you exemption from both federal and state income taxes. As you are holding the bonds for a more stable valuation, there is no point in owning a bond fund that invests in higher-risk bonds.

The highest quality bonds are rated "AAA," and bonds rated "AAA," "AA," and "BBB" are all considered investment-grade. Because the returns from bond funds are lower than with stocks funds, you need to pay particular attention to the expense ratios, which cut into returns proportionately more. You should be able to find satisfactory bond funds with expense ratios of three-quarter percent or less.

When selecting a bond fund, pay attention not only to yield but also the principal value. Some funds have a habit of paying back what is effectively your money as part of the yield in order to make the numbers look better. Managers might pay more than face value for high-yielding bonds and include some of that excess principal with the yields, gradually reducing the value back to face value.

While the intermediate term municipal bond fund average for 2008 was negative at -1.7 percent, the best-performing bond fund in this group made 3.5 percent, a value that has been fairly stable for years. This fund is the Fidelity Short-Intermediate Muni Income, symbol FSTFX. These funds are typically rated as a low risk.

Finally, as part of the basic holding, you will likely want to include some foreign or international stock exposure. It is easiest if you choose foreign rather than international, as your U.S. market exposure is already taken care of by your previous selection.

For a basic sound holding, avoid emerging markets and smaller companies and select a fund that invests in developed foreign markets and large-cap companies in the same way as your core U.S. stock holding.

The category of foreign stock funds as a whole had a dismal performance in 2008. The average return for this class of fund was -46 percent. However, the average included all sizes of company and countries. Nonetheless, you should expect a foreign large-cap growth or value fund to have lost about 40 percent in 2008, which is not an indication of a bad performer. One would hope that there will not be further significant deterioration in the price of these funds.

Adding Your Gainers

If you are comfortable taking risk, particularly when you have a longer time scale, I suggest putting 10 to 20 percent of your investment in more specialized funds, which carry the chance of much better returns. For instance, you may want to make an investment in emerging markets, especially in those that show promise. I would also include sector funds in this category, as they are not part of your sound medium-risk basic portfolio.

Many people at the moment are bullish on the health sector, pointing to the baby boomers, who are getting older and will have an increasing requirement for medical products of all kinds. The loss for the sector in 2008 was just 25 percent, which compares well to the standard investment funds. The best-performing health sector stock fund in 2008 was Fidelity Select Biotechnology (FBIOX), which is categorized as a high-risk fund with modest returns in previous years.

This is a prime example of how you cannot judge long-term performance solely on the basis of recent results. Another Fidelity fund, the Fidelity Select Medical Equipment/Systems (FSMEX), lost more than twice as much in 2008, yet trumps its sister fund soundly over the long-term with twice as much average return over the last ten years. While its risk rating is above average, this is still lower than a high-risk fund.

Particularly in the field of biotechnology and health care in general, there are numerous aspects and companies in which to invest. Biotechnology is not a specific product but rather is a field of study, thus it is possible to be invested in different companies, producing different goods for different sectors of the market, and still fall under the blanket title of biotechnology. Not surprisingly, different goods in different sectors of the health care market may have different fortunes and profit potentials; because of this, you can expect to find a wide fluctuation in the rewards of investing in biotechnology.

Do not consider a sector fund merely because many say it is a "hot" area. There is a self-fulfilling aspect to jumping onto the latest trend in that a certain proportion of the population will follow this and inevitably drive prices upward. But if there is not an increase in underlying worth then, as the trend cools, it is likely that sector will reduce its gains — or perhaps even start losing.

It is more sound to invest in a particular sector because you have done your research and realized it has the potential to grow. Even if the sector as a whole is expected to expand, as with the biotechnology example, you must be clear on what aspects of the sector are likely to prove worthwhile. Examine the fund's prospectus to see if the management aligns with your findings.

Depending on the amount of research you want to devote in a sector, you may even find it more worthwhile to invest in individual stocks that you have identified as particular growth companies. If you cannot find a sector mutual fund that takes your view of the market, this may be the only way you can participate in the high returns you believe are due. This is basic investing— more risky than diversifying through mutual funds — and is beyond the scope of this book. There is no shortage of information in the market about stock investment.

What If I Am In A 401(k) Plan?

If you are in a company-sponsored retirement plan, such as a 401(k), you will likely find that you are more limited in your choice of mutual funds. The retirement plans I have participated in have had a choice of ten or a dozen funds, preselected by the administrator. The administrator will give you choices among stock funds, bond funds, international funds, and some money market equivalent. Within the general categories, there may be a break down, such as into growth or value, or large cap or small cap.

With the knowledge you have gained from this book, you will be able to assess the quality of particular funds chosen within their sector or class. If they are in the top section of the performers for their class, they are acceptable, although you may not be receiving the best performance for your money. If they are near the bottom in their group, I would point this out to the fund administrator and ask that a different selection be made. You can also solicit the help of colleagues to bring pressure on those who choose the funds to make a change. It is in the interest of all members of the retirement plan to have access to funds that give a good performance.

Some companies will give you a selection of stock funds and, if you are not nearing retirement, you should have a substantial proportion of your 401(k) in stocks so you can partake of the better growth. You can use the basic principles outlined in this book to decide on the size of companies, the extent of foreign stocks, and other factors, and you can also look at the individual funds to ensure that you are not choosing one with a poor historic performance. For instance, you may find that a medium-cap stock fund gives better performance than the large-cap that is available to you, and it may demonstrate greater stability and less risk.

The bond funds will be the stable selection when you are concerned about the fluctuations of the stock market. For the younger investor, there is not a great need to put money in these funds. Though the value can fall when the interest rate rises, the extent of this depends on the term to maturity of the underlying bonds; at maturity, the full amount will be returned to the fund.

The money market fund option can be considered if you want security, but it has little to offer for the long-term investor, and there is no guarantee that the returns from a money market fund will even keep up with inflation. There is a technique to increase yield, explained in the next chapter, which involves a stable money market fund for easy access to your investment. Consider a money market fund if you want to try this approach.

Finally, a company-sponsored retirement plan may include the option of an Employee Stock Ownership Plan (ESOP). Again, this is somewhat outside the scope of this book, but if you have a chance to buy your company's stock at a discount, this may be valuable to you. Most advisors warn against investing too heavily in the company for which you work, as you already depend on it for your income and health plan. If the company goes into a decline, possibly resulting in layoffs, you do not want to lose some of your investment value, too.

Taking Action

If you have read this far, you are likely the type of person who will take action and review or start a healthy mutual fund portfolio. There is a lot of information in this book, and I advise you to re-read and make notes on items of specific interest. Follow through with the Internet sites mentioned to get up-to-date information on current details and performance, and use the companies' Web sites to confirm your decisions.

Mutual funds represent an easy way to tap into the markets' profits without needing to be obsessed with following the stock and bond world. You can outperform regular savings accounts and build your nest egg with little maintenance work once you have set up your portfolio. At the end of the day, it is your responsibility to take charge of your financial future, and using mutual funds represents one of the best ways to achieve that.

CHAPTER 13

Advanced Techniques to Increase Yield

Once you have assembled a portfolio, do not assume that you must leave it untouched for years in order to guarantee a good return. If you do not keep on top of your mutual fund selections, you are doing yourself — and your money — a disservice.

Admittedly, the "buy-and-hold" method appears to be effective when compared with what many do with their investments. Constantly chasing the latest tip, trading in and out of stocks, trying to squeeze the maximum returns, and otherwise churning their accounts is, for some, a way to convince themselves that they are working to get the returns. If you invest in stocks with a full-service stockbroker, you may be used to trading his recommendations often, and you may believe that is the best way.

Short-term trading, particularly of stocks but also in other financial markets, is a way that some people make a living, but the successful traders study hard and keep informed, and many would-be traders end up losing their money. Just because you keep busy with your holdings does not mean that you are adding value to them. In comparison with this scenario, "buy-and-hold" is an excellent strategy.

However, if you are prepared to work at your portfolio, you will find that you can increase the yields significantly over the person who makes excellent selections in the first place but neglects to pay attention to his or her account afterward. What you need to do is adopt a common-sense attitude regarding what you hold in your portfolio now and what you could be putting your money in, and achieve a balance that maximizes the potential.

Many people become attached to the portfolio that they have. After all, they took some time to make the initial selections, and it is hard to deviate from those; in their minds, to change the selections would imply that something was wrong with their original choices. This is far from the case, particularly with mutual funds whose performance can change from year to year. It makes good sense to review the portfolio at regular intervals and adjust the holdings for the best return. While a poorly performing fund may recover in time, during that time, you have lost the opportunity of making more money by investing in an excellent fund.

Dollar Cost Averaging

Dollar cost averaging is a method of continued investment that can smooth out fluctuations in the market automatically and ensure that investments continue to accumulate. The same principles apply whether you are investing in the stock market or increasing your mutual fund holdings by buying more mutual fund shares. Opinions vary as to how useful it is; whether it is regarded positively depends on your circumstances and the situation to which it is applied.

Quite simply, dollar cost averaging involves spending the same number of dollars at regular intervals to buy shares or stocks, regardless of their current price. This takes away the problem with market timing, in which you may find that you buy your shares at the peak of the market. Dollar cost averaging guarantees that you will not buy all the shares at their highest price — although, by the same logic, you will not buy all the shares at their lowest price.

An example will illustrate: Suppose you invest $1,000 every month in buying the shares that you have chosen. In the first month, the shares are valued at $10 each, the second month, $8 each, and the third month, $12 each. If you chose to buy all the shares at the beginning, using the $3,000 that you will spend over three months, you would about 300 shares.

If you decided to buy the shares using the dollar-cost-averaging system instead, the first month, you would buy 100 shares. As the price of the shares has fallen to $8 in the second month, your investment then will buy you 125 shares. By the time you get to the third month, the shares have increased in price to $12 each. Your $1,000 invested, then, will buy you 83 shares, plus a little change.

At the end of three months, with $3,000 invested, you would now own 308 shares, which is nearly 3 percent more than if you had bought all the shares on Day One. This is the strength of dollar cost averaging. However, note that if you had waited until the second month and realized that the shares were at a good value then, you would have been able to buy 375 shares. Given that it is difficult to time the market accurately, the dollar-cost averaging system is a simple, automatic method that will give you some advantage and protect you from the disadvantage that you might buy at the peak.

Value Averaging

An alternative to dollar cost averaging, which is more complicated but can produce better returns, is value averaging. Here, the idea is to invest to increase the value of your investments by a set amount per month. Again, this is a system you would apply when you are actively investing each month and looking to grow your portfolio. It can be used with any share holding, whether corporate or mutual fund.

In some respects, this method is more difficult to implement, as dollar cost averaging requires you to invest the same amount each month. On the other hand, value averaging may require you to find additional money to invest if the value of your fund's shares has fallen during the month.

In this way, the concept of how value averaging will improve your investing performance is easy to understand. For example, if the value of your fund has increased, you may not need to invest any money that month, and might even sell some shares and receive cash. Accordingly, when the fund's shares are expensive, you are not buying any more.

When the share value falls and you must find additional money to buy more shares and bring up the overall value of your holding, by this very action, you are buying when the shares are cheap. Thus, value averaging is an automatic method of buying low and selling high.

Combined Dollar Value Averaging

A further refinement of the above two methods combines them to overcome the difficulties with the value averaging that was noted. In this case, you will need two funds, one of which is a money market fund that gives you ready access to your cash. The other fund should be one that you expect to make greater gains, or a growth fund, which may have fluctuating values.

For this method, you invest a set amount each month, as noted in the dollar-cost-averaging method, which goes into the money market fund. So far, this is not different from the dollar cost method, as explained previously.

Where the value averaging method comes into this plan is with the growth fund. You apply the value averaging method to the growth fund and implement it as explained previously. The difference is that you use the money market fund as a source of money to invest the required amount each month or take out the profit, if necessary, and transfer it to the money market.

In this way, you are combining the regular setting-aside of money from your income, as required by the dollar-cost-averaging system, with the buying-low and selling-high feature of the value averaging system, thus forming a practical way to make best use of your regular investment.

Telephone Switching

If you are careful to select funds that do not impose switching fees, you may want to actively trade by using a telephone switching method. This means that you can use a phone to transfer money from one fund to another within the same investment company.

The telephone switching method requires you to follow the movement of the market and change funds when you see a different direction taking hold. This process entails that you take an active interest in your investments and the stock market, and has certain risks in consequence because even professional investors do not get it right all the time.

CASE STUDY: RICHARD E. REYES, CFP®

Richard Reyes carries through a football metaphor in his coaching business. He is an avid advocate of mutual fund investing.

The Financial Quarterback™/ Investor Coaching

"It has always been my belief to seek TRUTH. I believe in the saying that all growth starts with the TRUTH and that the TRUTH can set you free. In fact, I have spent a good deal of time questioning my assumptions and searching for the TRUTH.

The TRUTH I have discovered is that the term "financial planning" can be greatly misunderstood. In addition, investors want their money to accomplish their life's most important goals. The TRUTH is that a game plan with your personal investment objectives as the focal point is essential for you to feel success as an investor. For this reason, an amazing transformation occurred, and I created the Investor Coaching Experience.

I received my formal education at the University of Florida and completed the Certified Financial Planner Professional Education Program at the University of Central Florida. In addition to my professional qualifications, I am an active member of Junior Achievements, serve as a youth soccer coach for Florida Soccer Alliance, serve in several ministries with my church, and I am frequently asked to speak on various financial topics at numerous organizations. I also love to fly and am an accomplished commercial pilot."

Because of the time that he invests with his clients and his guiding coaching philosophies, Reyes has received many awards. He has been recognized in consecutive years by The Consumer Research Council of America, an independent Washington, D.C., research company that evaluates professional services throughout the United States, as one of "America's Top Financial Planners" in 2005, 2006, 2007, and 2008. In addition, Wealth and Business Planning Group LLC (The Financial Quarterback™), was chosen #24 in the prestigious Orlando Business Journal's 2007 Book of Lists as one of Central Florida's "Top 25."

Richard E. Reyes, CFP
100 E. Sybelia Ave., Suite 110
Maitland, FL 32751
P: 407-622-6669
F: 407-599-9243
Web: **www.thefinancialqb.com**
VLog: **www.thefinancialqb.comm/vlog**
E-Mail: richard@thefinancialqb.com

CASE STUDY: RICHARD E. REYES, CFP®

How did you get into the field of mutual fund investments?

Well, it was easy. I am an investor coach, and when I started in the business years back, I knew for certain that using mutual funds was the best and only prudent method for investors to use when investing in the stock market.

As a fund manager/investment adviser, what do you see as your primary function when selecting investments?

A dictionary will tell you that investing involves putting money into assets with the intent of making a profit, but that's not the whole story. Speculating, for example, involves the very same process.

So as an investor coach, it is important for me that our clients understand the difference between investing and speculating and, of course, eliminate speculating and gambling from their portfolio. This is often very difficult to do because, for the most part, the financial industry revolves around speculating and gambling, which makes billions for them, not the investor. So, due to the Wall Street marketing machine, many investors, even Wall Street, think they are investing, but they are speculating and gambling.

It is also important for clients to understand that if you are going to invest, you must allow the three most important factors of investing to work for you. Those three factors are that you must have time for the investment to work, put the power of compounding to work for you, and make sure that the investment can beat inflation over time.

As an investor coach, we help our clients make the prudent decisions about how much volatility and what types of risk they want to incorporate into their portfolios and distinguish prudent from imprudent risk. I also aid them to truly understand and measure diversification in the portfolio.

Given the current state of the financial markets, have you changed the way that you select any investments, or is your existing strategy already coping well?

Not at all, and because of the way we do things, our prudent and academic methods have been proven to work in any market or type of economy.

What do you like and dislike about mutual funds?

By definition, a mutual fund basically pools money together from thousands of investors, and then its managers buys stocks, bonds, or other securities with it.

CASE STUDY: RICHARD E. REYES, CFP®

From a diversification standpoint, a mutual fund can obviously assist with the process, but there are a lot of other issues to consider in order to put together a prudent portfolio.

Investors have to understand that there are three types of investors.

1) **Active**: Advocates of this approach believe that they are able to use a money manager or group of money managers who, together or individually, use some type of investment strategy or timing of the market in order to be able to try to "beat the market."

2) **Passive**: The passive approach believes that active managers have never proved that they were able to "beat the market" over time. In addition, those managers that have "beat the market" in certain times have done so due to luck rather than skill. Passive fund managers aim to replicate or track the movement of a particular benchmark index. Therefore, they will only trade securities when required to, in order to match the index that they are tracking. So its approach is to duplicate market rates of return rather than try to beat it.

3) **Hybrid**: This approach marries the active and passive approach.

Active versus passive management? The question is a controversial one and a central issue in the investment world. Active managers have no shortage of advocates.

My dislike of mutual funds is based on the use of actively managed mutual funds. Active fund managers aim specifically to manage a fund by achieving growth in excess of a benchmark index. They do this by stock picking or speculating on market movements and by actively trading securities within a fund. The manager of the actively managed fund now exposes the investor to very high fees and additional risk due to the constant trading of securities.

In addition, Wall Street is in the business of making money — a lot of money. If the performance of that fund is not up to par, or that particular fund is not attracting funds from investors, the investment company will get rid of the manager. A manager's tenure is usually less than three years. So when another manager comes in, his/her philosophy is always different, and the portfolio is thus changed once again, exposing the client to more fees and risk.

An actively managed fund does not enhance returns. High explicit charges, on the other hand, do have a strong and predictable negative impact upon net performance. So as you can see, Wall Street usually does not follow its own advice to invest in stocks for the long-term.

CASE STUDY: RICHARD E. REYES, CFP®

What personal qualities do you think help you succeed as a fund manager/investment adviser?

Investors must understand how investments work, especially what makes the markets work. In a nutshell, in a free, capitalistic society, the capital market rates of return are there for the taking. The basic underlying working mechanism of capital markets is to earn a return on your investment capital.

In addition, the investor must understand that no matter how well it has been designed and implemented, an investment strategy by itself can never bring you peace of mind. Although most of the financial world likes to pretend that investment decisions are based purely on logic and rational thought, the truth is that the vast majority of investment choices are driven by emotional and psychological factors.

So it is difficult sometimes, especially in a volatile economy, for an investor to marry the two concepts. So I have always felt that my job was to help the investor focus on their values and help them create a powerful vision of the future. So I bring a process that will help the investor get rid of the fear, anxiety, confusion, and complexity that most often surrounds the investing experience and keeps investors from staying disciplined.

What is the biggest success you have had concerning mutual funds?

Again, the use of passively managed funds allows us to design prudently diversified portfolios that expose our clients to portfolios that have more than 15,000 distinct securities, more than 15 different asset classes, spread over 39 countries. We use Modern Portfolio Theory to design and implement these portfolios, giving our clients broad exposure and a return that is in relation to a stated level of risk.

What is the biggest challenge that you have had to face?

It is hard to compete against the multi-trillion dollar marketing machine of Wall Street. Wall Street has done a superb job on getting the word out that actively managing your portfolio, trading in and out of the market, and market timing "works." Also, they continue to preach that you can simply just open up an account at TD Ameritrade® and trade stocks for a living, so this is somewhat ingrained into people's minds.

CASE STUDY: RICHARD E. REYES, CFP®

Nobel laureate Paul Samuelson stated "Wall Street gets paid to chase rainbows. The people on Wall Street just can't imagine how they would make a living if they weren't trying to beat the market."

What advice would you give to potential investors, particularly in the face of the economic crisis, and how would this vary depending on their age?

Get educated, get educated, get educated. You must understand investments and how they work. However, it is not as difficult as the financial industry makes it out to be. In addition, you can get as educated as you want, but you have to start. So get started, and keep educating yourself.

You always want to use a "fee-only" financial advisor (or investor coach) to work with and, hopefully, one that subscribes to passive investing. A fee-only advisor or coach takes no commissions and works for a firm that is not related to a brokerage firm, bank, or insurance company. A fee-only coach or advisor will make independent recommendations not based on commissions, but based on doing what is in your best interest.

What a fee-only coach or advisor does is to help you wade through all these very complex issues and maintain long-term discipline around the investing process because, ultimately, investing is a people problem, not necessarily a portfolio problem.

CHAPTER 14

How to Open an Account

Once you have selected the mutual fund you wish to purchase, you may be faced with several possibilities to open your account. If, as advised in this book, you choose to buy a no-load fund, you will either purchase it directly from the fund manager or use a discount broker, who will charge a flat rate.

The mutual fund company that you choose to invest your money with will have its own procedures, and some companies are more technically minded than others. You will have a choice of opening your account in the traditional way by requesting a printed application form that you can fill out and mail back, often including a check for your initial deposit. Some funds allow remote Internet application, and some fall between the two types, perhaps by having a downloadable application form that you must mail in.

Before you apply for an account, you still must make the decision regarding whether you will invest as a retirement account, or whether the account is for general funds. The next chapter delves into tax issues, a concept that is essential to understand at the outset; otherwise, you may find you are penalizing yourself financially.

To illustrate the process and the kind of information required, we will review a typical application form found online. These can vary in length from a couple of pages to perhaps eight pages including notes, and they are standard in the information they require. Often, the application form can be accessed on the Internet, allowing you to type your answers into set positions on the form and print it out for mailing. You likely cannot save the answers to your computer, as the form is locked, and once completed, you should print two copies — one to mail in and one for your records.

Laws require that you be provided with a prospectus for the fund you are interested in. If you are making the application online, the Web site will direct you to a download link from which you can receive an electronic copy of the prospectus and print at home. The company may ask you to confirm that you have received and read the prospectus before allowing you to open your account, and you may need to verify receipt of the prospectus by checking a box online before being permitted to apply.

The form begins with general information like your name, address, date of birth, and Social Security number. Federal law requires that the fund company be able to identify you, and these items are usually considered a minimum to satisfy that requirement. You will also be asked whether you are a U.S. citizen. On a form you can fill out electronically, you can simply click with your mouse in the "yes" box to insert a check mark.

The form will usually ask for home and business telephone numbers, and for your e-mail address. While these are not essential, they are for your own convenience. If the company has any questions, they will find it easier and quicker to contact you in one of these ways. You should see a disclaimer on the form that declares they will not use this information except in connection with your application.

At this stage, you will need to note whether the fund is in sole or joint ownership — for instance, if you wish to have your wife recorded as an owner on the account. You may be surprised to know that, if you have an individual account, not even a spouse is allowed access to it; upon your passing, the account would go into your estate and would need to pass through probate in order for the funds to become available to heirs.

To avoid probate, you may want to consider the type of ownership called Joint Tenants with Right of Survivorship. This is the usual choice offered for joint ownership, and you may have come across this term when you titled your house. This form of ownership allows both named people full access to the account, although you can require that checks need both signatures. Each person has an equal interest in the account, so if a divorce occurred, it would be split equally. The chief advantage is that if one owner dies, the other owner will automatically receive his or her share without going through probate. This would most often be used for a married couple, but other people may enter into this relationship and, as a rule, the mutual fund is deemed to be equally owned by all parties.

Another form of joint ownership, with two or more account owners, is called Tenants in Common. In this case, you are not restricted to equal proportions of ownership, and there is no transfer on death. The deceased's share would normally be part of his estate and would need to go through probate.

Another alternative exists if you want to open an account in your child's name, called a Transfer or Gift to a Minor. In this case, as the parent and custodian, you would need to fill out you and the minor's details, and the child would be entitled to access the fund upon reaching the age of majority. The age of majority varies from state to state, but is usually between 18 and 21. Any income from the account is reported as income to the minor.

Another form of ownership the form will ask about is whether there is a trust or other legal entity that will be involved. In this respect, you should consult your financial advisors to see whether you need to title the mutual fund holdings in a particular manner to suit your estate and asset management plan. For instance, you may have a living trust for the advantages that such an arrangement gives your heirs in the case of your death. Alternatively, you may have some corporate structure designed for asset protection.

Having established the legal ownership of the fund, the remaining section of the form is related to your investment. This will include details of your initial investment, and there will likely be a note on the form to remind you of the minimum amount required to open an account. The funds can be transferred in whatever way suits you. You can mail a check with the form or can arrange an electronic transfer from your normal bank account. The mutual fund may also receive an investment by transferring from another account at the same fund company or arranging to wire the money from an account.

If you want to invest in several funds from the same company, one way to make it easier is to put your initial investment in a money market fund account at the company. In this way, you can usually telephone the fund company and arrange a transfer to any of the company's other mutual funds, so it is easy to diversify your investment between several funds with only one transaction from your bank.

After the initial investment, the fund managers will likely give you several choices in how you can invest and withdraw funds. One method they encourage, and which I would recommend if it is appropriate for your situation, is setting up an automatic investment transfer at, say, monthly intervals. This authorizes the fund to request a regular amount from your bank account, and you can often say which day of the month you would like it withdrawn.

I recommend this method because it is often too easy to set up some form of investing and then neglect to fund it regularly. Often, unexpected bills arise, and they provide a convenient excuse for deciding that you cannot afford to save any money that month. While the most important step is actually opening a mutual fund account, to make something of your savings, you must invest regularly, and an automatic transfer will impose this discipline on you. I realize that in the current financial climate, it can be hard for many to commit to such a regime, but even if you find that you are withdrawing funds occasionally, the fact that they have been sent to the mutual fund in the first place provides some momentum to minimize your expenditures.

You can also set up an arrangement in which you can purchase or redeem funds by using an electronic funds transfer. The electronic funds transfer (EFT) may require you to send a blank check to the mutual fund company to share your checking account details. The blank check should be unsigned and voided. When you use this system to transfer, the funds goes through the same process as a check under the Automated Clearing House system, which can take a couple of days. Wiring money is faster but will usually be more expensive; however, the EFT is often free.

For a money market fund, you may have the choice of using checks to withdraw the money. This can be a useful facility, but pay attention to the minimum withdrawal amounts, which may be $250. This can be a convenient way to access your money if you think that you may need to make larger capital expenditures from time to time. By putting your savings into the fund, again, you activate the momentum of the money being there and needing to take action to withdraw it; over time, this will result in greater savings.

The form will then ask you to fill out what you want done with any dividends and capital gains. These can be reinvested into your fund or paid out in cash. If you are not depending on dividends for your living expenses, I would recommend making sure they are reinvested, as this will help improve the level of your savings.

These are the basic items you can find on any application form for a mutual fund investment. Once you have filled them out, all you must do is print it, sign the application, and submit it in accordance with the instructions.

Sometimes an application form may be used to apply for several different mutual fund holdings. In this case, the form may have a list of the different mutual funds available with that company, and you may need to check a box for the appropriate fund or fill in the amount that you want to invest there.

Opening a mutual fund account is an easy task and, if you can follow instructions, you will find the process simple with most, if not all, available funds.

Considerations for an IRA Account

You can use most mutual funds as the basis of an individual retirement account (IRA), but funds often require you to use a slightly different application form to ensure that the correct details are registered. You can only register a retirement account in one name; you do not have the facility of joint ownership. However, you can name primary and secondary beneficiaries to the account.

If you are opening a new IRA for your investment, you will need to specify the type of fund, such as traditional or Roth IRA. But there are limitations on how much you can fund it with each year. For the self-employed, there are options such as the Keogh plan that allow larger contributions, and you should consult with your accountant to make sure you set this up correctly. If you already have money in an IRA, you can obtain a form to transfer it to your new mutual fund IRA.

There are certain funds that you would probably not use in an IRA account, including tax-free municipal bond funds, which usually have a lower yield. In an IRA account, you do not pay tax until you start drawing the money at your retirement, so using these tax-free funds would be opting for a lower yield for no reason. You should also avoid choosing mutual funds that involve a high risk, as you will want to be sure that the money will be there for your retirement.

Using a Discount Broker

As I mentioned at the start of this chapter, instead of purchasing your no-load fund directly from the mutual fund company, you have a choice of using a discount broker and having access to hundreds of mutual funds. You might, for instance, use a discount broker if you are interested in trading or investing in individual stocks and bonds, as you could keep your complete portfolio in one account. Many people like to dabble in the stock market even if they are not committed to the more risky practice of trading. Buy-and-hold has not worked well recently for investors in individual stocks, but over the course of time, with sound selection and an occasional review, the stock market provides one of the best yields.

When using a broker, the application procedure is similar, although you may find that they ask more questions. One of the reasons for this is that a stockbroker will typically allow "trading on margin," a term for the individual investor borrowing some of the money needed for his investment from the broker. This permits the active trader to purchase a greater number of stocks with the intention of making a greater profit. To allow this process to occur, the broker will require details and a credit check. The broker also has a responsibility to assess whether you know what you are doing because of the risky nature of some investments you are able to make.

Before you consider buying mutual funds "on margin," be advised that the broker will charge you interest for using his money, so the additional rewards will not be great. If the funds go down in value at any time, not only will you lose more money by using a margin, but you may even find that the broker asks you for more money to cover the losses. This is called a "margin call." Finally, you cannot invest on margin in an IRA, which is where you should be investing most of your money for the future because of its tax advantages.

When you open your account, you can transfer any existing stocks, shares, and funds you hold into the account to keep everything in one place. The brokerage firm will be able to provide you with the appropriate forms, and they will take care of the transfer.

CHAPTER 15

Tax Issues

When you are trying to make money, the tax man is bound to take an interest. Investing in mutual funds may be no different from earning a salary or selling on eBay at a profit. On the other hand, it may be different because you do have options when you choose which mutual funds to invest in and how to invest in them. Tax situations with mutual funds can become complicated, but if you file your own taxes, you can likely deal with it. If you employ a tax professional each year at tax time, it may be wise to consult them when investing in mutual funds so that your account will be set up in the most advantageous way and you will be prepared for any taxes that come due.

If you are investing in mutual funds within a retirement account, tax would normally be due only when you take distributions, as with any other retirement investment. For this reason, you would want to select the fund that you judge will give the best payout within the asset class you are considering.

When investing in mutual funds outside a retirement fund, you will be liable for taxes on the profits and distributions. Depending on your tax bracket, you may find that a different type of fund might suit you better. For instance, if you are a high earner and expect to pay high taxes, consider whether tax-free bond funds might work better for you. As mentioned previously, these include government-issued bonds. Another choice for the high-tax-bracket investor are stock funds that give little or no dividend payouts, where your gains arise from capital appreciation. If you are in a low tax bracket, you should avoid tax-free bond funds because they usually have a lower return than taxable funds.

But even if you choose to have your distributions from the fund reinvested, you may still owe some income tax for the year, even if you have not done any dealing in the fund. The tax man looks at the distribution reinvestment as the same as if the fund paid you and you sent the money back to buy more shares.

There is no choice in this principle because the fund is required by law to distribute income and any capital gains that are realized by the manager selling stocks at a profit during the year. Indeed, if the fund did not distribute the additional money, the tax man would want to tax the fund directly, so you would still not escape paying taxes, albeit indirectly.

The question of the tax payable is an interesting one because even funds that seldom attract a capital gain do sometimes sell stocks, and the fund manager is responsible for deciding whether the fund to invest in will do so. Therefore, you are not able to say with certainty how much tax liability you will incur in any particular year.

The only way to be sure of the tax payable is to opt for a municipal bond fund. The income from this fund will be free of federal taxes, and if you choose a bond issued in the state where you pay taxes, it will usually be free from state taxes as well. However, you must figure in the rate of return that you can expect when deciding whether this is the best course.

If all this talk of paying taxes is troubling you, take it as an indication that your long-term savings should take advantage of any tax-deferred options that are available to you. This would include a 401(k) plan or an IRA. Your accountant will be able to advise you on the maximum amount that you can contribute to these each year.

After you have contributed all that is allowed to these types of accounts, you may want to consider a mutual fund that is termed "tax-managed." You will find that an increasing number of mutual funds fit into this category; for example, Vanguard offers a variety of them in different investment forms. The manager of a tax-managed fund will try to limit the taxable events, such as capital gains, that occur in the fund. When he sells for a profit, he may realize some losses in another part of the fund at the same time in order to reduce any tax liability. This is no guarantee in terms of how much tax you will have to pay, but you can be sure it is a concern of the fund management.

Notice that it is not a good plan to put tax-managed funds into a tax-deferred account, such as a traditional IRA. The fund manager aims to avoid capital gains distributions, which would minimize your tax liability. When you cash in the fund, you will be liable for tax at the capital gains rate. If these funds are held in a traditional IRA, all withdrawals are taxed at your income tax rate, which almost inevitably will be higher than your capital gains rate.

Another way to minimize the taxes that you pay on any distributions, whether or not they are reinvested, is to look carefully at all your investments and see whether some have lost money. If you can identify funds or other investments that are worth less than they cost you and you think they will not perform well, then you can sell them to realize the capital loss. This amount can be offset against your income, reducing the tax that you owe.

The IRS allows you to use up to $3,000 of capital losses each year to offset your income tax and, if you have greater than $3,000 in losses, the excess is carried forward to future years. There used to be a loophole in this strategy, in which you could sell at a loss to obtain a tax write-off and then buy back the investment if you believed it was going to start performing better; that way, you would establish the loss for tax purposes, but not lose out on any gains in the fund.

But when this trick was discovered, the rules changed. You are now not allowed to buy back the same fund within 30 days of selling it, or you will lose your tax write-off. This prevents you from buying back the same fund if you want to have the tax advantage, but there is no restriction on your purchasing a similar fund that invests in the same way as the one you sold, if you think that particular market sector is poised to make gains.

With the advent of the Roth IRA, your calculations of what type of fund to buy and what kind of account to hold it in became somewhat more complicated. As a reminder, the Roth IRA is different from a traditional IRA in that your money is taxed before it is invested, but qualified withdrawals from the Roth IRA are tax-free. The traditional IRA works the other way around, with the investment being tax deductible — i.e., tax-free — but the qualified withdrawals are taxed at your income tax rate at the time, such as at retirement.

If you are prepared and qualified to open a Roth IRA account, it makes sense for this to hold funds that are expected to make large returns because no matter how large the return, no tax will be due. Therefore, if you have any stock-based funds, which historically achieve the largest returns given a sufficiently long holding period, they should be held in a Roth account.

Working with the Tax Forms

Having revealed that you may be liable for some tax on your fund even if you have not benefited from it or touched it, I should add that you must not worry unduly about figuring this out. Your mutual fund company or broker will send you the necessary forms containing the information required to fill out your tax return.

If you do your own tax return, perhaps using software like Taxcut or TurboTax, then you must simply answer the appropriate questions when you fill out that section of the information by supplying the numbers given to you on the form. If you use a tax preparer, he or she should be familiar with the mutual fund form, which you would give them with your other papers.

At this stage, you may be interested to know how many different forms you will receive — and when. You will receive a tax form for any taxable income distributed by the fund, for any switching of funds, and for any redemptions that you made. You should receive the forms by the end of January, but if you do not have them within a couple of weeks after this date, call the mutual fund and report that they are missing, as the fund can issue duplicates. These tax forms are also provided to the IRS, so they will be informed already of the amounts that you have received.

The forms you will receive are all 1099 forms with different suffixes, depending on the purpose. Even if you have not held a mutual fund before, you have likely received a 1099 form from your bank. For savings accounts and CDs, the bank would likely issue you a 1099-INT, which details the interest earned on those accounts. The form is relatively simple, including blanks for your name and address, the issuer's name and address, some identification numbers, and separate numbered boxes for various amounts to be noted.

If you earned more than $10 in dividends or capital gains distributions, you should receive a 1099-DIV form from the mutual fund. You will receive this even if you have the dividends reinvested automatically.

If you redeemed shares or exchanged them in the previous year, you should receive a form 1099-B. As I will explain later, this form cannot give you all the information needed for the taxes involved, but it summarizes the transactions.

When you have a retirement account, such as an IRA, and you receive a distribution from it, you will receive the form 1099-R.

You may also report non-IRA account distributions on the same form using different boxes.

The forms are reproduced here for your use. Because they are not created by Federal employees, they are not subject to copyright; however, these copies are for informational purposes only and do not conform to the scannable standards required by the IRS and, therefore, cannot be used or substituted for the official forms. Using copies of these forms in a return may result in a penalty of $50.

The official scannable forms are available from the IRS by calling 1-800-TAX-FORM or by applying online at **www.irs.gov**. This is likely an unnecessary step, as the fund is responsible for providing the forms to you, filled out with the appropriate values.

1099-DIV

	CORRECTED (if checked)		
PAYER'S name, street address, city, state, ZIP code, and telephone no.	1a Total ordinary dividends $	OMB No. 1545-0110 **2009** Form 1099-DIV	**Dividends and Distributions**
	1b Qualified dividends $		Copy B For Recipient
	2a Total capital gain distr. $	2b Unrecap. Sec. 1250 gain $	
PAYER'S federal identification number	RECIPIENT'S identification number	2c Section 1202 gain $	2d Collectibles (28%) gain $
		3 Nondividend distributions $	4 Federal income tax withheld $
RECIPIENT'S name			5 Investment expenses $
Street address (including apt. no.)		6 Foreign tax paid $	7 Foreign country or U.S. possession
City, state, and ZIP code		8 Cash liquidation distributions $	9 Noncash liquidation distributions $
Account number (see instructions)			

This is important tax information and is being furnished to the Internal Revenue Service. If you are required to file a return, a negligence penalty or other sanction may be imposed on you if this income is taxable and the IRS determines that it has not been reported.

Form 1099-DIV (keep for your records) Department of the Treasury - Internal Revenue Service

Instructions for Recipients

Account number. May show an account or other unique number the payer assigned to distinguish your account.

Box 1a. Shows total ordinary dividends that are taxable. Include this amount on line 9a of Form 1040 or 1040A. Also, report it on Schedule B (Form 1040) or Schedule 1 (Form 1040A), if required.

The amount shown may be dividends a corporation paid directly to you as a participant (or beneficiary of a participant) in an employee stock ownership plan (ESOP). Report it as a dividend on your Form 1040/1040A but treat it as a plan distribution, not as investment income, for any other purpose.

Box 1b. Shows the portion of the amount in box 1a that may be eligible for the 15% or zero capital gains rates. See the Form 1040/1040A instructions for how to determine this amount. Report the eligible amount on line 9b, Form 1040 or 1040A.

Box 2a. Shows total capital gain distributions from a regulated investment company or real estate investment trust. Report the amounts shown in box 2a on Schedule D (Form 1040), line 13. But, if no amount is shown in boxes 2c–2d and your only capital gains and losses are capital gain distributions, you may be able to report the amounts shown in box 2a on line 13 of Form 1040 (line 10 of Form 1040A) rather than Schedule D. See the Form 1040/1040A instructions.

Box 2b. Shows the portion of the amount in box 2a that is unrecaptured section 1250 gain from certain depreciable real property. Report this amount on the Unrecaptured Section 1250 Gain Worksheet–Line 19 in the Schedule D instructions (Form 1040).

Box 2c. Shows the portion of the amount in box 2a that is section 1202 gain from certain small business stock that may be subject to a 50% exclusion and certain empowerment zone business stock that may be subject to a 60% exclusion. See Schedule D (Form 1040) instructions.

Box 2d. Shows 28% rate gain from sales or exchanges of collectibles. If required, use this amount when completing the 28% Rate Gain Worksheet–Line 18 in the instructions for Schedule D (Form 1040).

Box 3. Shows the part of the distribution that is nontaxable because it is a return of your cost (or other basis). You must reduce your cost (or other basis) by this amount for figuring gain or loss when you sell your stock. But if you get back all your cost (or other basis), report future distributions as capital gains. See Pub. 550, Investment Income and Expenses.

Box 4. Shows backup withholding. For example, a payer must backup withhold on certain payments at a 28% rate if you did not give your taxpayer identification number to the payer. See Form W-9, Request for Taxpayer Identification Number and Certification, for information on backup withholding. Include this amount on your income tax return as tax withheld.

Box 5. Shows your share of expenses of a nonpublicly offered regulated investment company, generally a nonpublicly offered mutual fund. If you file Form 1040, you may deduct these expenses on the "Other expenses" line on Schedule A (Form 1040) subject to the 2% limit. This amount is included in box 1a.

Box 6. Shows the foreign tax that you may be able to claim as a deduction or a credit on Form 1040. See the Form 1040 instructions.

Box 7. This box should be left blank if a regulated investment company reported the foreign tax shown in box 6.

Boxes 8 and 9. Shows cash and noncash liquidation distributions.

Nominees. If this form includes amounts belonging to another person, you are considered a nominee recipient. You must file Form 1099-DIV with the IRS for each of the other owners to show their share of the income, and you must furnish a Form 1099-DIV to each. A husband or wife is not required to file a nominee return to show amounts owned by the other. See the 2009 General Instructions for Forms 1099, 1098, 3921, 3922, 5498, and W-2G.

The 1099-DIV Form and Instructions

This is the form you should receive if you have held any mutual funds in the previous year that made any money. It is similar to the W-2 form that you receive from your employer each year. The quantities entered on the form are in boxes that are numbered and labeled, so these are easy to understand and enter yourself if you do your own taxes.

Assuming that your name and address are correct, the first box you should be interested in is called *1a Total ordinary dividends*. The distributions that are included as ordinary dividends are taxed at your highest tax rate, which — if you are a higher-rate taxpayer — can be significant. This box includes not only dividends, but also short-term capital gains distributions — those capital gains that the fund manager realized from buying and selling securities held in the fund. However, the dividends do not include those paid by stocks held in the fund; rather, only dividends from money market and bond holdings are included.

The next box, *1b Qualified dividends*, is where you will find the amounts paid out as dividends on the stocks held in the mutual fund. This is due to a change in the tax laws a few years ago, in which stock dividends are taxed at a reduced rate and called "qualified dividends."

The third box is also somewhat confusingly labeled, called *2a Total capital gain distribution*. As I pointed out when looking at box 1a, short-term capital gains are included there, so box 2a contains only long-term capital gains, not total gains as implied by the name. You may know that long-term capital gains are taxed at a lower rate than short-term capital gains, and this applies whether the securities were held by you in your name or held in a mutual fund, as in this case. The definition of long-term capital gains is the profit made by selling securities that have been held for more than 12 months.

You should not see numbers in many of the following boxes. If you see anything in box 4, for instance, which is called "federal income tax withheld," there may be a problem, as this indicates you are subject to backup withholding. This might happen if your Social Security number is incorrectly recorded. You will need to check this with the IRS, and you should receive a credit for this tax, already paid when you submit your tax return.

Another place where you may occasionally find a number is in *Box 6 Foreign tax paid*. If you have an internationally based mutual fund, the fund may have paid necessary foreign taxes on the dividends. You are allowed to claim at least part of these back from the IRS, and you can either claim a dollar-for-dollar reduction in your taxes by putting the number on the foreign tax credit line of your tax return Form 1040, or, if you itemize your deductions, you can include them in your Schedule A, putting them on the "other taxes" line.

1099-B

☐ CORRECTED (if checked)

PAYER'S name, street address, city, state, ZIP code, and telephone no.	1a Date of sale or exchange	OMB No. 1545-0715	Proceeds From Broker and Barter Exchange Transactions
	1b CUSIP no.	**2009** Form 1099-B	
	2 Stocks, bonds, etc. $	Reported ☐ Gross proceeds to IRS ☐ Gross proceeds less commissions and option premium	
PAYER'S federal identification number	RECIPIENT'S identification number	3 Bartering $	4 Federal income tax withheld $	**Copy B For Recipient** This is important tax information and is being furnished to the Internal Revenue Service. If you are required to file a return, a negligence penalty or other sanction may be imposed on you if this income is taxable and the IRS determines that it has not been reported.
RECIPIENT'S name	5 No. of shares exchanged	6 Classes of stock exchanged	
Street address (including apt. no.)	7 Description		
City, state, and ZIP code	8 Profit or (loss) realized in 2009 $	9 Unrealized profit or (loss) on open contracts– 12/31/2008 $	
CORPORATION'S name	10 Unrealized profit or (loss) on open contracts–12/31/2009 $	11 Aggregate profit or (loss) $	
Account number (see instructions)	12 If the box is checked, the recipient cannot take a loss on their tax return based on the amount in box 2 ☐ ------		

Form 1099-B   (keep for your records)   Department of the Treasury - Internal Revenue Service

Instructions for Recipients

Brokers and barter exchanges must report proceeds from transactions to you and the IRS on Form 1099-B. Reporting is also required when your broker knows or has reason to know that a corporation in which you own stock has had a change in control or a substantial change in capital structure. You may be required to recognize gain from the receipt of cash, stock, or other property that was exchanged for the corporation's stock. If your broker reported this type of transaction to you, the corporation is identified in the box below your name and address on Form 1099-B. Account number. May show an account or other unique number the payer assigned to distinguish your account.

Box 1a. Shows the trade date of the transaction. For aggregate reporting, no entry will be present.

Box 1b. For broker transactions, may show the CUSIP (Committee on Uniform Security Identification Procedures) number of the item reported.

Box 2. Shows the aggregate proceeds from transactions involving stocks, bonds, other debt obligations, commodities, or forward contracts. May show the proceeds from the disposition of your interest(s) in a widely held fixed investment trust. Losses on forward contracts and changes in control or substantial change in capital structure are shown in parentheses. This box does not include proceeds from regulated futures contracts. The broker must indicate whether gross proceeds or gross proceeds less commissions and option premiums were reported to the IRS. Report this amount on Schedule D (Form 1040), Capital Gains and Losses. However, if box 12 is checked, you cannot take a loss on your tax return based on gross proceeds from an acquisition of control or substantial change in capital structure reported in box 2. Do not report this loss on Schedule D (Form 1040). The broker should advise you of any losses on a separate statement.

Box 3. Shows the cash you received, the fair market value of any property or services you received, and/or the fair market value of any trade credits or scrip credited to your account by a barter exchange. See Pub. 525, Taxable and Nontaxable Income, for information on how to report this income. any property or services you received, and/or the fair market value of any trade credits or scrip credited to your account by a barter exchange. See Pub. 525, Taxable and Nontaxable Income, for information on how to report this income.

Box 4. Shows backup withholding. Generally, a payer must backup withhold at a 28% rate if you did not furnish your taxpayer identification number to the payer. See Form W-9, Request for Taxpayer Identification Number and Certification, for information on backup withholding. Include this amount on your income tax return as tax withheld.

Box 5. Shows the number of shares of the corporation's stock that you held which were exchanged in the change in control or substantial change in capital structure.

Box 6. Shows the class or classes of the corporation's stock that were exchanged in the change in control or substantial change in capital structure.

Box 7. Shows a brief description of the item or service for which the proceeds or bartering income is being reported. For regulated futures contracts and forward contracts, "RFC" or other appropriate description may be shown.

Regulated Futures Contracts:

Box 8. Shows the profit or (loss) realized on regulated futures or foreign currency contracts closed during 2009.

Box 9. Shows any year-end adjustment to the profit or (loss) shown in box 8 due to open contracts on December 31, 2008.

Box 10. Shows the unrealized profit or (loss) on open contracts held in your account on December 31, 2009. These are considered sold as of that date. This will become an adjustment reported in box 9 in 2010.

Box 11. Boxes 8, 9, and 10 are all used to figure the aggregate profit or (loss) on regulated futures or foreign currency contracts for the year. Include this amount on your 2009 Form 6781.

The 1099-B Form and Instructions

This is the form you will receive if you have redeemed any of your funds or switched between funds, which the IRS views as redeeming and buying the other fund. As mentioned, this form gives you only part of the story, and you or your financial advisor are responsible for determining the rest of the information that the IRS needs to confirm your tax liability.

What the 1099-B form does, however, is provide a reminder of all the sales and transactions that you need to account for on your tax form and, again, this is copied to the IRS and should not be ignored.

If you have sold any funds in the previous year, you will need to calculate your capital gain or loss and determine your tax liability. You also must report this for your tax-free funds. To determine your gains or losses, you must calculate what the IRS terms the basis of your holding. This represents the net cost of the holding to you, which provides a baseline that shows the levels of gains or losses you have experienced from having the fund.

It helps if you have kept your records from when you bought your funds originally and your statements that show dividend reinvestments each year. If you have not, you may have some additional work to do to find these numbers. You can start by calling the mutual fund company and asking them for copies of the statements, and you may also find that the mutual fund company can tell you your average cost per share in the fund. Because your account will have been purchasing shares from reinvestments each year, this is the simplest way to find out the basis of your holding.

If you are selling all your shares in the fund at one time, that information should be sufficient; if you are selling only a portion of your shares, there are other methods of looking at the basis for your holding, which will result in different tax liabilities. And if you choose to use one of these methods, you will need to continue with it when selling the rest of your holding. Depending on how you look at the basis, you may find that you reduce your tax liability for the sale, but may increase your liability when you sell the rest of the fund. As you may anticipate being in a different tax bracket in the future, or believe that the tax rates are changing in a certain direction, you can choose the method that you want to use accordingly. If you use a financial consultant and the fund amounts are not large, it might cost you more for the consultant to perform these calculations than you will save in the taxes.

The first method of valuing your funds is called the specific identification method. In this case, you nominate which of your mutual fund shares you are selling, whether it be your original investment, subsequent investments, or shares bought with dividend reinvestment. You can take any combination you want of these.

If you want to use this method, you should direct your fund company at the time of sale to which shares you are selling. For instance, you might have asked to sell 100 shares that you bought on a certain date or for a certain price. The IRS does not ask for this information when you file your taxes but, if you are audited, you will need to produce the evidence. Remember that if you nominate the shares that you bought at the highest price, perhaps most recently, then you will minimize your taxes for this transaction; however, your taxes when you next sell will be calculated based on the cheaper purchase price of the remaining shares.

If you did not direct your fund based on which shares you were selling when you sold only part of your holding, then the IRS may tell you that you need to use the "first-in, first-out method," otherwise known as FIFO. The name of this method explains how you determine the basis for your capital gain calculation. Whichever shares you bought first will be the ones that are considered sold first. If you have your records of all the shares, including those that were added by reinvestment, you can start at the beginning, allocating shares and continuing until you reach the number that you have cashed in, most likely finishing up with part of a purchase.

This method is straightforward, provided you have your records or can obtain them, and it guarantees that the oldest are considered sold first. Thus, it will automatically ensure that you will be taxed on long-term capital gains — if possible — before the short-term gains, which are taxed at a higher rate.

Finally, even for the sale of part of your mutual fund shareholding, you can elect to use the average cost method. Note that you will need to stick with the same method when you sell later shares, so your election at this point fixes the method of valuation for the future.

Once you have the cost basis of the shares you have sold, this provides the missing information that you need to fill out your tax return. The information on the 1099-B form is a declaration of how much money you sold the shares for, so combining the two sets of numbers gives you the capital gain, or capital loss, figure for the transaction.

1099-R

☐ VOID ☐ CORRECTED		
PAYER'S name, street address, city, state, and ZIP code	1 Gross distribution $	OMB No. 1545-0119 **2009** Form 1099-R	Distributions From Pensions, Annuities, Retirement or Profit-Sharing Plans, IRAs, Insurance Contracts, etc.
	2a Taxable amount $		Copy 1 For State, City, or Local Tax Department
	2b Taxable amount not determined ☐	Total distribution ☐	
PAYER'S federal identification number RECIPIENT'S identification number	3 Capital gain (included in box 2a) $	4 Federal income tax withheld $	
RECIPIENT'S name	5 Employee contributions /Designated Roth contributions or insurance premiums $	6 Net unrealized appreciation in employer's securities $	
Street address (including apt. no.)	7 Distribution code(s) ☐ IRA/ SEP/ SIMPLE	8 Other $	
City, state, and ZIP code	9a Your percentage of total distribution %	9b Total employee contributions $	
1st year of desig. Roth contrib.	10 State tax withheld $ $	11 State/Payer's state no.	12 State distribution $ $
	13 Local tax withheld $ $	14 Name of locality	15 Local distribution $ $
Account number (see instructions)			

Form 1099-R   Department of the Treasury - Internal Revenue Service

Instructions for Recipient

What is new. If any of the distribution relates to your economic stimulus payment, see the instructions for Form 1040 or 1040A. Generally, distributions from pensions, annuities, profit-sharing and retirement plans (including section 457 state and local government plans), IRAs, insurance contracts, etc., are reported to recipients on Form 1099-R.

Qualified plans. If your annuity starting date is after 1997, you must use the simplified method to figure your taxable amount if your payer did not show the taxable amount in box 2a. See the instructions for Form 1040 or 1040A.

IRAs. For distributions from a traditional individual retirement arrangement (IRA), simplified employee pension (SEP), or savings incentive match plan for employees (SIMPLE), generally the payer is not required to compute the taxable amount. See the Form 1040 or 1040A instructions to determine the taxable amount. If you are at least age 701/2, you must take minimum distributions from your IRA (other than a Roth IRA). If you do not, you may be subject to a 50% excise tax on the amount that should have been distributed. See Pub. 590 for more information on IRAs.

Roth IRAs. For distributions from a Roth IRA, generally the payer is not required to compute the taxable amount. You must compute any taxable amount on Form 8606. An amount shown in box 2a may be taxable earnings on an excess contribution.

Loans treated as distributions. If you borrow money from a qualified plan, section 403(b) plan, or government plan, you may have to treat the loan as a distribution and include all or part of the amount borrowed in your income. There are exceptions to this rule. If your loan is taxable, Code L will be shown in box 7. See Pub. 575.

Account number. May show an account or other unique number the payer assigned to distinguish your account.

Box 1. Shows the total amount you received this year. The amount may have been a direct rollover, a transfer or conversion to a Roth IRA, a recharacterized IRA contribution; or you may have received it as periodic payments, as non-periodic payments, or as a total distribution. Report the amount on Form 1040 or 1040A on the line for "IRA distributions" or "Pensions and annuities" (or the line for "Taxable amount"), and on Form 8606, as applicable. However, if this is a lump-sum distribution, see Form 4972. If you have not reached minimum retirement age, report your disability payments on the line for "Wages, salaries, tips, etc." on your tax return. Also report on that line permissible withdrawals from eligible automatic contribution arrangements and corrective distributions of excess deferrals, excess contributions, or excess aggregate contributions except if you are self-employed.

If a life insurance, annuity, or endowment contract was transferred tax free to another trustee or contract issuer, an amount will be shown in this box and Code 6 will be shown in box 7. You need not report this on your tax return.

Box 2a. This part of the distribution is generally taxable. If there is no entry in this box, the payer may not have all the facts needed to figure the taxable amount. In that case, the first box in box 2b should be checked. You may want to get one of the free publications from the IRS to help you figure the taxable amount. See additional information on the back of Copy 2. For an IRA distribution, see IRAs and Roth IRAs above. For a direct rollover, other than from a qualified plan to a Roth IRA, zero should be shown, and you must enter zero (-0-) on the "Taxable amount" line of your tax return. If you roll over a distribution (other than a designated Roth account contribution) from a qualified plan (including a governmental section 457(b) plan) or section 403(b) plan to a Roth IRA, you must include on the "Taxable amount" line of your tax return the amount shown in this box plus the amount in box 6, if any.

If this is a total distribution from a qualified plan and you were born before January 2, 1936 (or you are the beneficiary of someone born before January 2, 1936), you may be eligible for the ten-year tax option. See the Form 4972 instructions for more information.

Box 2b. If the first box is checked, the payer was unable to determine the taxable amount, and box 2a should be blank. If the second box is checked, the distribution was a total distribution that closed out your account. If you are an eligible retired public safety officer who elected to exclude from income distributions from your eligible plan used to purchase certain insurance premiums, the amount shown in box 2a has not been reduced by the exclusion amount. See the instructions for Form 1040 or Form 1040A for more information.

Box 3. If you received a lump-sum distribution from a qualified plan and were born before January 2, 1936 (or you are the beneficiary of someone born before January 2, 1936), you may be able to elect to treat this amount as a capital gain on Form 4972 (not on Schedule D (Form 1040)). See the Form 4972 instructions. For a charitable gift annuity, report as a long-term capital gain on Schedule D.

Box 4. Shows federal income tax withheld. Include this amount on your income tax return as tax withheld, and if box 4 shows an amount (other than zero), attach Copy B to your return. Generally, if you will receive payments next year that are not eligible rollover distributions, you can change your withholding or elect not to have income tax withheld by giving the payer Form W-4P.

Box 5. Generally, this shows the employee's investment in the contract (after-tax contributions), if any, recovered tax free this year; the portion that is your basis in a designated Roth account; the part of premiums paid on commercial annuities or insurance contracts recovered tax free; or the nontaxable part of a charitable gift annuity. This box does not show any IRA contributions. If the amount shown is your basis in a designated Roth account, the year you first made contributions to that account may be entered in the box next to box 10.

Box 6. If you received a lump-sum distribution from a qualified plan that includes securities of the employer's company, the net unrealized appreciation (NUA) (any increase in value of such securities while in the trust) is taxed only when you sell the securities, unless you choose to include it in your gross income this year. However, if the distribution was a qualified rollover contribution to a Roth IRA, see the instructions for Box 2a. See Pub. 575 and the Form 4972 instructions. If you did not receive a lump-sum distribution, the amount shown is the NUA attributable to employee contributions, which is not taxed until you sell the securities.

Box 7. The following codes identify the distribution you received. For more information on these distributions, see the instructions for your tax return. Also, certain distributions may be subject to an additional 10% tax. See the instructions for Forms 5329 and 8606.

1 — Early distribution, no known exception (in most cases, under age 59½).

2 — Early distribution, exception applies (under age 59½).

3 — Disability.

4 — Death.

5 — Prohibited transaction.

6 — Section 1035 exchange (a tax-free exchange of life insurance, annuity, or endowment contracts).

7 — Normal distribution.

8 — Excess contributions plus earnings/excess deferrals (and/or earnings) taxable in 2009.

9 — Cost of current life insurance protection.

A — May be eligible for 10-year tax option (see Form 4972).

B — Designated Roth account distribution.

D — Excess contributions plus earnings/excess deferrals taxable in 2007.

E — Excess annual additions under section 415 and certain excess amounts under section 403(b) plans.

F — Charitable gift annuity.

G — Direct rollover of a distribution (other than a designated Roth account distribution) to a qualified plan, a section 403(b) plan, a governmental section 457(b) plan, or an IRA.

H — Direct rollover of a designated Roth account distribution to a Roth IRA.

J — Early distribution from a Roth IRA, no known exception (in most cases, under age 59½).

L — Loans treated as distributions.

N — Recharacterized IRA contribution made for 2009 and recharacterized in 2009.

P — Excess contributions plus earnings/excess deferrals taxable in 2008.

Q — Qualified distribution from a Roth IRA.

R — Recharacterized IRA contribution made for 2008 and recharacterized in 2009.

S — Early distribution from a SIMPLE IRA in first 2 years, no known exception (under age 59½).

T — Roth IRA distribution, exception applies.

U — Dividend distribution from ESOP under sec. 404(k).

Note. This distribution is not eligible for rollover. If the IRA/SEP/ SIMPLE box is checked, you have received a traditional IRA, SEP, or SIMPLE distribution.

Box 8. If you received an annuity contract as part of a distribution, the value of the contract is shown. It is not taxable when you receive it and should not be included in boxes 1 and 2a. When you receive periodic payments from the annuity contract, they are taxable at that time. If the distribution is made to more than one person, the percentage of the annuity contract distributed to you is also shown. You will need this information if you use the 10-year tax option (Form 4972).

Box 9a. If a total distribution was made to more than one person, the percentage you received is shown.

Box 9b. For a life annuity from a qualified plan or from a section 403(b) plan (with after-tax contributions), an amount may be shown for the employee's total investment in the contract. It is used to compute the taxable part of the distribution. See Pub. 575.

Boxes 10–15. If state or local income tax was withheld from the distribution, boxes 12 and 15 may show the part of the distribution subject to state and/or local tax.

Additional information. You may want to see:

Form W-4P, Withholding Certificate for Pension or Annuity Payments

Form 4972, Tax on Lump-Sum Distributions

Form 5329, Additional Taxes on Qualified Plans (Including IRAs) and Other Tax-Favored Accounts

Form 8606, Nondeductible IRAs

Pub. 560, Retirement Plans for Small Business (SEP, SIMPLE, and Qualified Plans)

Pub. 571, Tax-Sheltered Annuity Plans (403(b) Plans)

Pub. 575, Pension and Annuity Income

Pub. 590, Individual Retirement Arrangements (IRAs)

Pub. 721, Tax Guide to U.S. Civil Service Retirement Benefits

Pub. 939, General Rule for Pensions and Annuities

Pub. 969, Health Savings Accounts and Other Tax-Favored Health Plans

The 1099-R form and instructions

As mentioned at the start of this section, this form is issued if you have taken any withdrawals from a retirement fund. From a tax point of view, you will not want to do this before you are 59½ unless you have particular extenuating circumstances. Because you did not pay tax on the money when it was invested, the IRS will charge you a penalty for taking the money out early and a tax at the current rate on the amount you withdraw.

The retirement account is kept untouched because the money was not taxed and the gross amount is increasing in value. If you have also made another equivalent investment after paying income tax, you would only have growth on the net amount, which would be less. Therefore, you can use your other investment accounts first before tapping into the qualified retirement account.

There are exceptions to the minimum-age rule. You still must pay income tax on the withdrawal; there can be no exception to that because the money in an IRA has never been taxed, but you may be able to escape the additional penalties. These exceptions include reasons of particular hardship or need:

- Your medical expenses are more than 7.5 percent of your income.
- The withdrawal was court ordered.
- The money is needed for higher education.
- The money is to buy a first time home.
- You stopped work after you turned 55.
- The money is needed because of a disability.
- The money was paid out because of death.

Another point to consider when making withdrawals from a retirement account is that you must be careful to start making them before you reach the age of 70½, when you have a certain minimum amount you must withdraw to avoid large tax penalties. You need to check with your financial advisor to ensure that you comply with this requirement, who will be able to tell you how much you must take out. The only exception is if your retirement account is a Roth IRA, in which there is no required distribution.

The form 1099-R is similar to other 1099s, with numbered boxes to help you identify the different amounts to report on your tax return. The retirement account distributions tend to be taxable because tax was not paid on the amounts when they were invested. Check the names, addresses, and identification numbers carefully to be certain that the copy of the form, which will have been sent to the IRS, can be matched up to your tax return.

The first amount that is of interest to you is in *box 1 Gross distribution*. Look at this amount to make sure it is the same as the sum you withdrew from your IRA. This will normally be fully taxable with a standard IRA, in which you paid no tax on the contributions.

The second box, *2a Taxable amount*, will likely be the same, but note that this may not be correct. It may be the best information that the payer of the distribution has, but its accuracy depends on how you contributed to the IRA.

It is possible that you made some contributions that were not deductible for tax purposes, but are the person who would know about that — not necessarily the fund manager. If you did make such contributions, you must fill out a Form 8606 and attach it to your return.

If your retirement account is not an IRA, but a Keogh, 401(k), or SEP-IRA, then your tax treatment may be different. The amount reported on the 1099-R should be transferred to your tax return. If you contributed to the fund with money that is subject to tax at the time, then, in principle, there will be less tax liability on the gross distribution you received.

With plans that are not IRAs, you may find amounts in some of the other boxes. For instance, *box 3 Capital gain* may apply if you participated in the plan before 1974. *Box 4 Federal income tax withheld*, if it has a value, represents tax that is already deducted, and you will get credit for this payment when you complete your tax return.

Box 5 deals with contributions you have made in which you did not get tax deductions, such as for a Roth plan, and 6 covers securities in your employment, which will be taxed only when you sell them. Box 7 is an explanation of why you are receiving the distribution and, if 8 and 9 have values, you may need to consult a tax specialist.

If you are confused by the above explanations, then your financial advisor should be consulted, as the intent of this book is not to provide detailed specialist tax advice, but rather general guidance on matters affecting mutual funds.

GLOSSARY

12b-1 Fees: Fees paid out of a fund to cover the costs of selling shares and sometimes some costs of shareholder services.

Account Fee: Fee sometimes charged to investors toward the account maintenance costs. For instance, there may be a fee charged if your account goes below a certain dollar value.

American Association Of Individual Investors: An independent non-profit organization that, for more than 30 years, has provided education and research for investing individuals.

Backend Load: A charge that some mutual funds make when you sell their shares, which is generally used to pay brokers.

Board of Directors: The Board of Directors oversees the fund's administration and protects the interests of the shareholders.

Bond Fund: A fund that invests in bonds.

Bond: A certificate for a company's or government's debt.

Class: Used to distinguish between different types of shares issued by a mutual fund. A fund may issue Class A shares and Class B shares, for example. While the investment portfolio will be the same for all these shares, there may be different shareholder services or fees associated with the different classes.

Closed-End Fund: A type of mutual fund investment in which all the shares are sold at one time and subsequently traded on an exchange.

Contingent Deferred Sales Load: A form of backend load in which the actual charge depends on the length of time the investor has held the shares.

Conversion: With some mutual funds that offer several classes of ownership, conversion from one class to another can occur if the investor has been invested for a certain period of time.

Country Fund: The same as a single-country fund; a fund that invests in one country.

Coupon: Another word for the dividend or yield of a bond.

Deferred Sales Charge: The same thing as the backend load; see above.

Derivative: A financial instrument that is derived from another.

Distribution Fees: Fees required to sell the shares; see 12b-1 Fees above. These include expenses such as advertising costs and prospectuses.

Diversification: Investing in different sectors and types of securities with the purpose of minimizing the risk of a fall in value in one area affecting all of your investment.

Emerging Market Fund: A fund that invests in a growing market.

Enhanced Index Fund: A fund that is based on an index, but invested to perform differently — for instance, to achieve twice the gain of the index.

Equity Fund: A fund that invests in equities or stocks.

Exchange Fee: The fee charged by some mutual fund companies if investors want to change to another fund in the same company.

Exchange Fund: An exchange fund allows capital gains from one investment to be rolled into the next for tax purposes, so tax is only paid when the last investment is sold.

Exchange-Traded Funds: A type of investment, similar to a mutual fund, aimed at providing the same return as a particular market index.

Expense Ratio: The total expenses for operating a fund,

expressed as a percentage of the money invested.

Feeder Fund: A fund that invests in another fund.

FIFA: First-in, first-out — a method of determining the basis of a shareholding for tax purposes.

Foreign Fund: A foreign fund invests only outside the country of domicile.

Front End Load: A front end load is a charge some mutual funds make to buy shares, which is generally used to compensate the brokers who sell the shares.

Fund Administrator: The fund administrator has the overall charge of making sure that the fund complies with legal requirements.

Fund of Funds: A fund that invests in other mutual funds.

Futures: A contract to purchase something, often a commodity, in the future.

Global Fund: A fund that is not limited to investing in the US.

Growth Fund: A fund that concentrates on capital gain in making investments.

Hedge Fund: A type of fund for sophisticated investors that often uses derivatives to accelerate returns — not a mutual fund.

Incubated Fund: A method of testing a potential mutual fund before formally creating it.

Index Fund: a type of mutual fund that seeks to emulate the performance of an index, such as the S&P 500 or the Dow Jones Industrial Average.

International Fund: A fund that invests only overseas.

Investment Adviser: An investment adviser usually receives money for giving individual advice to investors. Often, the investment adviser refers to the company that employs the manager.

Investment Advisers Act: A law passed in 1940 regulating the actions of investment advisers.

Investment Advisor: A person qualified by study and examination to assist you in your investment choices.

Investment Company Act: A law governing the operation of an investment company.

Investment Company: A company that issues securities and primarily invests in other securities with the money received, such as a mutual fund company.

Large Cap: Short for large capitalization; refers to the largest value companies.

Life-Cycle Fund: A fund in which the investments are changed over time to suit an anticipated date for redemption.

Load Fund: A fund in which a load is charged; see Load.

Load: A sales charge, otherwise known as a front-end load, which you may be charged for buying a share in a mutual fund.

Management Fee: A management fee is paid to an investment advisor who is in charge of the securities bought by the fund.

Market Index: Same as an index; this refers to a basket of

securities and the combined value worked out according to a formula — for example, the Dow Jones Industrial Average.

Master Fund: Refers to a fund that buys other funds.

Medium-Cap: Refers to medium-size companies.

Money Market Fund: A fund that invests to maintain the capital while giving a modest return.

Multi-Advisor Fund: A multi-advisor fund with several managers.

Mutual Fund: A collective fund of investors' money, also a common name for the investment company — that is, a company that attracts money from investors and deposits the money in other securities in the hope of getting a good return to pay to the investors. Mutual funds issue shares that can be bought directly from the company, as opposed to having to buy them on a securities market.

NASD: Short for the National Association of Security Dealers, a self-regulatory organization for the securities industry, now merged with the Financial Industry Regulatory Authority.

Net Asset Value (NAV): This is the value of a fund's assets, less the liabilities of the fund. This is commonly quoted as per share by summing the fund's assets less liabilities and dividing by the number of shares that have been issued.

No-Load Fund: A fund that does not charge a sales fee. Note that there may be other charges in a no-load fund, as well as the operating expenses that are charged by all funds.

Open-End Fund: A fund with no restriction on new investment.

Operating Expenses: The costs to run a fund, including management fees, distribution fees, and expenses.

Options: A financial derivative that allows the buyer the option of buying a security in the future for a certain price.

Portfolio: The collection of shares, bonds, and other securities held by an individual or by a fund.

Prospectus: The document required by law that describes a mutual fund for potential shareholders and investors. As described in the section on the prospectus, certain facts must be included in the prospectus.

Purchase Fee: An additional fee charged by some funds for buying their shares; not necessarily the same as a front end load.

Real Estate Investment Trust: An organization that invests in real estate.

Redemption Fee: A fee charged by some mutual funds when an investor wishes to redeem his shares. Not necessarily the same as a backend load. The maximum fee is limited by the SEC to 2 percent.

Regional Fund: A fund that invests in a certain area or region of the world.

SAI: Short for Statement of Additional Information, which is further information about a mutual fund that is not required to be given to investors unless requested. It is also known as Part B of the registration.

Sales Charge: Another word for load; the amount investors are charged to buy or redeem their shares in the mutual fund. This is not limited by the SEC, but the NASD requires that sales loads not exceed 8.5 percent.

SEC: Short for the Securities and Exchange Commission, the government body that protects investors and regulates the financial industry.

Sector Fund: A fund that makes investments in a certain type of security — for instance, energy.

Shareholder Service Fees: Fees payable by shareholders in return for answers to inquiries.

Shareholders: The shareholders own the fund and can vote, just as with shares in any company. They can appoint to the Board of Directors and may be involved in approving other matters.

Single-Country Fund: A fund that invests in one country.

Small Cap: Small companies.

Sub-Advised Fund: A fund that uses advisors from other companies.

Switching Fees: Fees charged for changing from one fund to another.

Target Risk Fund: A fund that maintains a certain risk.

Target-Date Fund: A fund that aims to give the best return at a certain date while avoiding excess risk as the date approaches.

Targeted-Distribution Fund: A fund in which the dividends are stated and anticipated.

Tax-Free Fund: A fund that makes investments that do not attract tax.

Tracker Fund: Another name for an index fund.

Transfer Agent: The transfer agent is employed by the fund company & keeps shareholder records, sends out dividends and tax information, and performs related functions.

Value Fund: A fund in which the managers look for undervalued companies in which to invest.

World Fund: A fund in which the managers consider investing in any company in the world.

BIBLIOGRAPHY

Benz, Christine. *Morningstar Guide to Mutual Funds -- Five Star Strategies for Success* (John Wiley & Sons Inc., 2005)

Gerber, Melinda. *How to Create and Manage a Mutual Fund or Exchange Traded Fund -- a Professional's Guide* (John Wiley & Sons, Inc., 2008)

Jacobs, Bruce. *All About Mutual Funds* (McGraw-Hill, 2001)

Tyson, Eric. *Mutual Funds for Dummies* (Wiley Publishing Inc., 2007)

BIOGRAPHY

Alan Northcott is a successful financial author, freelance writer, trader, professional engineer, and farmer, along with other pursuits, and he now lives in the Midwest. Originating from England, he immigrated with his wife to America in 1992. His engineering career spanned more than 30 years, on both sides of the Atlantic, and recent years have found him seeking and living a more diverse, fulfilling life style.

This is his fourth financial book, and his previous works are also available from Atlantic Publishing. He offers a free newsletter on various related topics. You can find out more at **www.alannorthcott.com**, or e-mail him directly at **alannorthcott@msn.com**.

INDEX